"This incredible book is the perfect bala_____, a pastor of a church in South Florida where _____ are represented, knows how to connect with t_____ the heart to love people and to reach them. And he has the academic prowess to know how to guide challenging biblical conversations. I commend highly his book, *Persuasive Apologetics: The Art of Handling Tough Questions Without Pushing People Away*."

—Dr. Thom S. Rainer,
Founder and CEO, Church Answers;
Author, *I Am a Church Member*

"Consider this volume a one-size-fits-all text, which is not surprising considering that Jeff Robinson is a pastor with an earned PhD. Accordingly, this book moves from why apologetics is needed to worldviews, methodology, particular tactics, answers to world religions, the problem of evil, and the believer's final hope of eternity. After all, if Christianity is true, it ought to be applied in very practical ways! Check it out—highly recommended!"

—Dr. Gary R. Habermas,
Distinguished Research Professor,
Liberty University, Lynchburg, Virginia

"This book is smart, succinct, punchy, and persuasive. Jeff Robinson draws from such far-flung fields as martial arts, modern movies, popular video games, prominent philosophers, and the wisdom of Scripture. The result: an impressive array of intellectual weapons trained on the target of disbelief, along with solid answers to help any thinking person consider trusting in Christ. Read it for yourself, but put it into action for the sake of others."

—Mark Mittelberg,
Executive Director of the Lee Strobel Center
for Evangelism and Applied Apologetics;
Author, *Confident Faith* and *Contagious Faith*

"*Persuasive Apologetics* fulfills a vital need in the apologetics literature—namely, to bridge rigor of a reasoned defense on behalf of the Christian faith with relevance and meaning to the person being persuaded. More so than in times past, people do not simply want to follow a line of argument as an amusing intellectual exercise, but they want to know why it should matter to them given their own life experience and situation. This book helps apologists for the Christian faith make that connection between the rational and the personal."

—Dr. William A. Dembski,
Distinguished Fellow, Bradley Center for Natural and Artificial Intelligence
Author, *The Design Inference*

"With winsomeness, style, and irenic grace, Jeff Robinson offers a theologically rich, rhetorically informed, and compelling Christian apologetic that hits just the right note by taking seriously the importance of *how* apologists communicate. In divisive and tendentious times, fresh approaches to apologetics are vitally needed, and Robinson's is one among a number of emerging voices committed to lowering the contention quotient, generating healthy discussions, and building bridges in an effort to win people, not just arguments."

—Dr. David Baggett,
Professor of Philosophy and Director of the Center for Moral Apologetics,
Houston Christian University, Houston, Texas

"If you've been waiting to launch your journey into apologetics, your patience just paid off. Jeff Robinson defines our task as 'loving people by addressing their questions in an intellectually rigorous yet gentle and respectful manner.' Robinson's conversational style makes this book a reading pleasure even as he drops learned nuggets left and right. Preparing to deliver an apology for the faith is required of all Christians, and *Persuasive Apologetics* is the best place I know for the general believer to begin."

—Dr. Malcolm B. Yarnell III,
Research Professor of Theology,
Southwestern Baptist Theological Seminary, Fort Worth, Texas

"Dr. Robinson has linked the heart of a pastor with the mind of a theologian in *Persuasive Apologetics: The Art of Handling Tough Questions Without Pushing People Away*. He provides an incredible tool for applied apologetics for believers seeking to navigate the complexities of culture. I highly recommend this writing on the academic and personal level for individuals desiring to grow in their Christian faith."

—Dr. Tommy Green,
Executive Director,
Florida Baptist Convention

"Jeff Robinson is a seasoned scholar and skilled apologist. But he is also a pastor of a multiethnic, multigenerational church in one of the great mission fields in North America. He draws on this experience to create a fun, warm, rich reading experience. This book offers believers a solid foundation for Christian apologetics in an accessible format. Christians will be encouraged and challenged to be more confident and intentional about having gospel conversations."

—Dr. Jimmy Scroggins,
Lead Pastor,
Family Church, West Palm Beach, Florida

"The need to be able to fairly understand the objections of unbelievers, confidently defend our faith, and lovingly share it without turning people off has never been greater or more challenging than it is right now. That's why I think you should check out Jeff Robinson's book, *Persuasive Apologetics: The Art of Handling Tough Questions Without Pushing People Away*. It will give you the foundations for understanding how to defend your faith and knock out the props holding up false worldviews; but even more importantly, it will equip you to be a witness in a world desperate for redemption in Jesus Christ, even if it doesn't know it yet."

—Dr. Jon Akin,
Vice President for Church Relations and Campus Ministries,
Carson-Newman University, Jefferson City, Tennessee

"In a conversational style, Robinson takes his readers through the introductory elements of the world of Christian apologetics. Interacting with leading Christian apologists, he guides his readers through the necessary questions of method and tone, while also illustrating how to respond to a number of common objections to Christian theism. Robinson thus provides a helpful introduction to the world of apologetics, while pointing his readers to numerous ways to go deeper in their contention for truth."

—Dr. A. Chadwick Thornhill,
Director of Graduate Biblical and Theological Studies Programs,
Associate Professor of Apologetics and Biblical Studies,
John W. Rawlings School of Divinity, Liberty University, Lynchburg, Virginia

"Apologetics is always in need of application. Those convinced by the truth need a tool to communicate it. This is why Jeff Robinson's *Persuasive Apologetics* is such a gift. It allows one to grapple with the arguments with an end toward putting it into practice. I highly recommend it!"

—Dr. Steven Smith,
Professor of Preaching and Pastoral Ministry,
Senior Preaching Fellow, Spurgeon Library,
Midwestern Baptist Theological Seminary, Kansas City, Missouri;
Senior Pastor, Immanuel Baptist Church, Little Rock, Arkansas

"Do not miss the word *Art* in the title of Jeff Robinson's book. He does excellent work with the science of apologetics. However, it is the *art* of handling the tough questions that makes this book rise to excellence. No true Jesus follower wants to push people away from the gospel. This book will help you win the person and not just an argument. I wholeheartedly commend my former intern's book to you."

—Dr. Ted Traylor,
Senior Pastor, Olive Baptist Church, Pensacola, Florida

"Rev. Dr. Jeff Robinson has provided a wonderfully accessible and engagingly relatable treatment of apologetics. Though he proves his philosophical and theological mettle with his words, he makes an even greater, pastoral contribution to apologetics with his emphasis on love. If the apologist doesn't love her discussion partner, then her arguments fall flat. There is much to be enjoyed and appreciated in this volume. I am honored to recommend it!"

—Dr. Earl Waggoner,
Dean and Professor of Theological Studies,
Colorado Christian University, Lakewood, Colorado

"Jeff Robinson has answered the call to present an accessible manual on apologetics, drawing from a deep well of having a scholar's mind and pastor's heart. This is no mere academic presentation from a nonpracticing professor. It is a great tool from a practitioner who has taken key principles of apologetics and translated them to the turf and trenches of real-life ministry, where he does his best work. Jeff has done a fine job taking apologetics from concept and theory to practice and even action."

—Dr. Bernie Cueto,
Vice President for Spiritual Development,
Palm Beach Atlantic University, West Palm Beach, Florida

"*Persuasive Apologetics* is a great tool for raising up the next generation of faithful witnesses in a society in desperate need of Christian witness. Robinson's writing is engaging in life application, deep in intellect, and compelling in expression. Robinson brings biblical thinking to bear on the major questions of faith in contemporary society with philosophical precision and clarity about everyday living. Every high schooler, college student, young adult, and those in the church who work with them should read this book."

—Dr. Jon Wood,
Vice President for Student Life and Christian Ministries,
Cedarville University, Cedarville, Ohio

"*Persuasive Apologetics* will catch you off guard. Jeff Robinson has the unique ability to write about apologetics in a delightfully engaging way. He presents Christian apologetics without apology. He stands firm in his defense of the faith, yet with grace and kindness. His writing reminds us that apologetics and kindness are not mutually exclusive. I guarantee you will be glad you took the time to read this book."

Dr. Doug Randlett,
Senior Associate Pastor,
Thomas Road Baptist Church, Lynchburg, Virginia

"Having served as a professor of evangelism for the past fifteen years, I want to commend Dr. Jeff Robinson for his timely book. If you care about our world and the need for the truths of the gospel to prevail, then you must read this book! Know that while Dr. Robinson is eminently qualified as an academician, everything he approaches in life, including this book, is filtered through the heart of a local church pastor. His aim is not to impress you with his intellect but to help bring an unsaved world to redemption through the good news of Jesus Christ."

—Dr. David A. Wheeler,
Professor of Evangelism and Senior Executive Director of LU Shepherd,
John W. Rawlings School of Divinity, Liberty University, Lynchburg, Virginia

"*Persuasive Apologetics: The Art of Handling Tough Questions Without Pushing People Away* is a much-needed work for our harsh world today. With a perfect blend of humor, practical application, and scholarly depth, author Jeff Robinson delivers a resource that will help you hone your skills in giving a reasoned defense for the hope that lies within us, delivering it with grace and humility."

—Dr. James Peoples,
Director, Send Network Florida,
North American Mission Board

"*Persuasive Apologetics: The Art of Handling Tough Questions Without Pushing People Away* is a much-needed book for our times. The book is both scholarly and practical with touches of humor that make reading the book both profitable and enjoyable. I strongly endorse Dr. Robinson's book and highly recommend it as an introductory textbook in apologetics at the university level as well as for small group study and discussion for thoughtful laypeople in the church."

—Dr. Ken Mahanes,
Retired Dean of the School of Ministry,
Palm Beach Atlantic University, West Palm Beach, Florida

"I have known Jeff Robinson for many years, and I have watched him consistently direct his intellectual and spiritual gifts toward the building up of Christ's church. He continues that trajectory with this book, writing an accessible but important piece. *Persuasive Apologetics* will benefit readers who are interested in defending their faith; it is a fun and accessible introduction to Christian apologetics."

—Dr. David Rathel,
Associate Professor of Christian Theology,
Gateway Seminary, Fremont, California

"Written with a pastor's heart and an academic's focus, *Persuasive Apologetics* offers the reader an opportunity to interact with material both funny and fundamental. Robinson reflects on the need for apologetics in the Christian life while addressing key issues related to apologetic foundations and approaches. With a sense of humor and an understanding of some key academics in the field, Robinson provides an engaging text that provides what it promises. You don't have to be an academic to understand it, but if you are a Christian, you will benefit from it. If you've ever wondered how to defend your faith while providing a robust account for the hope of Christ that is in you, then this book is a good foundation."

—Dr. Leo Percer,
Director, PhD in Theology and Apologetics Program,
Associate Professor of Biblical Studies,
John W. Rawlings School of Divinity, Liberty University, Lynchburg, Virginia

"*Persuasive Apologetics* is a fun and engaging primer on understanding the strong intellectual and biblical foundations of the Christian faith. Dr. Robinson writes with a pastor's heart. His depth of knowledge and compassion shine on every page. New and seasoned Christians will greatly benefit from this book."

—Dr. Mark Moore,
Assistant Professor of Theology,
William Jessup University, Rocklin, California

"As it's possible to win a battle and lose the war, it's also possible to convince someone of a position and lose their trust. In *Persuasive Apologetics*, Jeff Robinson provides a toolkit for both thinking strategically about arguments and caring deeply for people. This volume includes a clear explanation of essential apologetic issues alongside a consistent focus on the techniques and ethics of persuasion. Warmly recommended."

—Dr. Ched Spellman,
Associate Professor of Biblical and Theological Studies,
Cedarville University, Cedarville, Ohio

"Jeff Robinson has given the church and the academy a gift in *Persuasive Apologetics*. Writing with a pastoral heart, a conversational style, and an academic mind, Robinson writes an engaging introduction to the apologetic task. I highly recommend *Persuasive Apologetics* to students and lay people who want to answer tough questions related to the Christian faith in a manner that reflects the grace and seriousness of the gospel."

—Dr. James M. Todd III,
Associate Professor of Biblical and Theological Studies,
College of the Ozarks, Point Lookout, Missouri

"This book is both powerful and practical in its aim at providing biblical insight into our Great Commission mandate 'for such a time such as this.' Jeff Robinson is the pastor of a great multiethnic, multicultural, and multigenerational church in South Florida that is a perfect reflection of what heaven will look like. His leadership, experience, and passion to reach people from every walk of life is felt in *Persuasive Apologetics: The Art of Handling Tough Questions Without Pushing People Away*. I highly recommend his book."

—Patrick D. Coats,
Black Multicultural Catalyst,
Florida Baptist Convention

"As the field of apologetics seems to be drifting further away from the average Christian to a more academic discipline, *Persuasive Apologetics* is a much-needed reminder of just what apologetics is: a call to defend the faith that was once and for all delivered to the saints. Dr. Robinson takes us back to our roots of all Christians defending the faith. He reminds us that apologetics is not some obscure, esoteric, and rarefied field of scholarship that is only for the likes of learned doctors and cave-dwelling Christian yogis. At the heart of apologetics is the simple truth that every Christian is an apologist, able to take on the Goliaths of ignorance and secularism with the smooth stones of truth, love, and a Spirit-filled life. *Persuasive Apologetics* will challenge you to put your faith on display and defend the joyful hope of the Christ-life with gentleness and respect."

—Dr. Stan Lewis,
Lead Pastor,
First Baptist Crestview, Crestview, Florida

"This wonderful book is a winsome consideration of an important topic: how to be ready to give an account for our gospel hope while also loving God by loving others. I recommend highly that you carefully read and learn from *Persuasive Apologetics: The Art of Handling Tough Questions Without Pushing People Away*. The book is both engaging and clear while also loving and gracious. Jeff Robinson, who pastors a multicultural church in South Florida, has given us an important contribution to our current cultural conversation. Importantly, I have observed Jeff to be a loving, capable witness of his faith as commended in these pages. This is truly worth your time."

—Don R. Cockes,
Regional Catalyst,
Southern Baptist Convention of Virginia

PERSUASIVE APOLOGETICS

THE ART OF HANDLING TOUGH QUESTIONS WITHOUT PUSHING PEOPLE AWAY

JEFFREY M. ROBINSON

Persuasive Apologetics: The Art of Handling Tough Questions Without Pushing People Away

© 2023 by Jeffrey M. Robinson

Published by Kregel Academic, an imprint of Kregel Publications, 2450 Oak Industrial Dr. NE, Grand Rapids, MI 49505-6020

ISBN 978-0-8254-4830-0

Printed in the United States of America

23 24 25 26 27 / 5 4 3 2 1

To my precious wife and children—
I love you.

CONTENTS

FOREWORD

It was one of those days you won't forget. Indeed, it was one of those days you don't want to forget.

I made the drive across the peninsula of Florida from Bradenton to West Palm Beach. The lead pastor of Grace Fellowship: A Church for All the Nations asked me to do an onsite mini-consultation. My purpose was to look at the church facilities, to see the surrounding communities, and to offer any insights I could within the short timeframe of the consultation.

But there was another major component of the consultation. I had the incredible opportunity to listen to the lead pastor, Jeff Robinson, for several hours. I guess I asked a few questions and responded to Jeff's questions. But the real treat was hearing from the heart of the pastor who loved his church, the members of the church, and the community where they lived.

The simple summary of my one-day journey was profound. I heard how God was working in a place where many people said no to God and said no to churches. I heard God's yes to a church in South Florida. I heard how the gospel of Christ was reaching thousands through this church. I heard how seventy-two different first-generation nations are represented in this church today.

Jeff knows that residents of South Florida, like people all over the world, have questions about God and faith—lots of questions.

Jeff knows how to communicate God's truth to them. He knows how to answer their questions and demonstrate the love of Christ. Grace Fellowship has followed the lead of their pastor. The members are likewise reaching a diversity of people from incredible backgrounds, ethnicities, and nations.

I entered into this consultation wondering how I could help this church. I prayed that God would give me the wisdom to say the words I need to say. But I returned to Bradenton with the keen awareness that I was not the conveyor of wise words. Jeff and his church did not hear from me as much as I heard from God.

The questions are obvious. How did he do it? Even better, how did God do it through this pastor and this church? How did the seemingly impossible become possible? People have asked Jeff those questions countless times. Now, we have a book that tells us how.

This incredible book is the perfect balance of mind and heart. Jeff Robinson, a pastor of a church in South Florida where seventy-two first-generation nations are represented, knows how to connect with the world and culture. He has the heart to love people and to reach them. And he has the academic prowess to know how to guide challenging biblical conversations. This book, *Persuasive Apologetics: The Art of Handling Tough Questions Without Pushing People Away,* will introduce a new wave of apologetics and evangelism to those who truly desire to reach a lost and hurting world.

It's a book, but it is so much more. It is the story of God's work. And it is nothing less than the story of God's miraculous powers at work today.

—Dr. Thom S. Rainer
Founder and CEO, Church Answers
Author, *I Am a Christian*

ACKNOWLEDGMENTS

This book was made possible with the help of more people than I can name. My church family, Grace Fellowship: A Church for All Nations—with seventy-two first-generation nations represented at the time of writing—serves as a beautiful example of a community rigorously and graciously engaging a plethora of worldviews. I owe a debt of gratitude to our elders, who have encouraged this project. Thank you for your kingdom perspective. To our pastors and directors, it's an honor serving with you.

To my parents, I cannot fully express my gratitude for your sacrifice on my behalf. Your example of engaging with ideas formed my love for reading and learning at a very early age. Although I may not have fully appreciated it then, thank you for not allowing me to squander my childhood in front of screens and video games. See this volume as a testament to your commitment to training your children in the Scriptures.

To my colleagues, professors, and ministry mentors, our countless discussions continue to be invaluable over the years. Your willingness to lend an ear to my ideas means more than you know. Thank you for sharpening me. I owe a debt of gratitude to the universities and professors that are including this book in their courses. I am also grateful for churches who have found this text useful for group discipleship ministry. All of the proceeds from this book are allocated to the ministry of Grace Fellowship: A Church for All Nations in order to reach Palm Beach County, South Florida, and the world with the Good News of Jesus Christ.

To the top-grade academics who are still in the trenches of frontline ministry work, you are my heroes. To the local church ministers who, with the purpose of loving people well, resist intellectual stagnation and continue to read peer-reviewed publications (thus enduring the eye rolls of those who do not consider such things "practical"), you inspire me. Press on.

To my beautiful wife and the world's best editor, you are a precious gift from God and a genuine Proverbs 31 woman. Your selflessness and ability to dialogue about numerous arcane topics humble me. You are genuinely an indescribable blessing.

To our sons, you are young as I write this, but I pray you grow to be men of God. May our innumerable imaginary battles against Philistines, pirates, and bad guys, with the help of our beloved heroes (Beowulf, David's mighty men, and King Jan Sobieski, with his winged hussars), translate to a lifelong calling to defend the defenseless and never forsake the battle for truth. Be courageous, and know that your father will always stand shoulder to shoulder with you for what's right.

Finally, I am thankful to God for the indescribable riches of his grace. Without his work in my life, I would still be spiritually dead and without hope. My prayer is that this book will assist Christians in removing intellectual roadblocks to the gospel while being sensitive to the leading of the Holy Spirit when interacting with those who may not yet believe. To God be the glory.

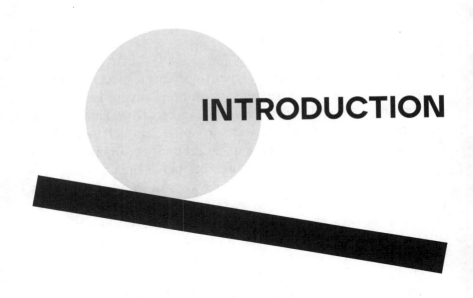

INTRODUCTION

We are not merely imperfect creatures who must be improved; we are, as Newman said, "rebels who must lay down our arms."

—C. S. Lewis, *The Problem of Pain*

When it comes to academic writing, specificity is the name of the game. A three-hundred-plus-page dissertation can focus on what sort of flea colony was living in Gottfried Leibniz's third dog and its relevance to his unfinished monograph on what could have led to a breakthrough in seventeenth-century Flemish higher calculus to the degree of . . . you get the picture. Academics is all about focus, and that's a good thing. It's how we add to the body of scholarly knowledge. It's how we avoid rabbit trails and hone our ability to think well. Behind most successful and timeless popular-level books or films sits the scholar. There is always a "mind behind."

Whether or not we realize it, we are indebted to the scholarly community of men and women who have dedicated their lives to studies that, to be frank, elicit yawns from many of us. I am grateful for committed scholars. The person whose life is dedicated to seeking truth or the good, whether elusive philosophical proofs or a cure for debilitating illnesses, is worthy of our respect. A willingness to self-assess and, if need be, discard one's hypotheses if they are shown to be lacking distinguishes thinkers from fanatics who happen to have a degree next to their name. True scholars follow the evidence and resist the urge to cancel their opponents.

This book, however, is a bit different. Rather than a hyper-specific academic monograph, it is an overview of some of our time's pressing faith questions. Whereas my past writings have been laser-focused, this work casts a wide net because, outside the ivory towers of academia, we often do not have the luxury of tightly focused conversations about our faith. It is quite simply the world in which we live. Therefore, I intend to give you *the essentials to be an effective witness for Christ and nothing more.* I'll save the other stuff for future writing projects where we can really geek out together. Yes, we'll walk through some historical nuggets and philosophical handles, but only as they relate to the task of guiding others to a warranted confidence in Jesus Christ. Our focus will be broad because of the vast scope of pushback points in our present world.

Just a heads-up: The first three chapters deal with foundational or "basement" stuff. We will talk about why we should do apologetics and how to use apologetic tactics, the power of a person's worldview presuppositions, the importance of our demeanor in being persuasive, and how to combine these tools into a versatile and eclectic approach. If you are new to apologetics and find sections of this book a bit dense, let not your heart be troubled. Intentional illustrations are planted at (hopefully) strategic points to help refocus what may at first seem abstract. It's not until chapter 4 that we get into the meat of doing apologetics in a direct fashion. The heart of this book is twofold: understanding that there is often more that lurks below intellectual-sounding objections to Christianity, and developing the ability to use undercutting defeaters to destabilize opposing worldviews. This is all with the aim of reaping a greater evangelistic harvest through the tools and methods that God has ordained.

For his glory,
Jeff

CALL OF DUTY (NOT THE VIDEO GAME)

I am not a gamer, unless you count pre-internet-era afternoon sessions of *Duck Hunt* and *Super Mario Bros.* at a friend's house while trying to drown out the sound of Mom's TV in the other room as she watched *As the World Turns*. I'm actually too afraid to try gaming at this stage in life simply because I may like it. If I were to like it, I would most certainly fail life as a whole. It's a margin thing. But I do remember when *Call of Duty* first hit the market. Friends, colleagues, and family members devoured it like pepperoni pizza at a Baptist youth lock-in. But beyond all the tactics, fanfare, and less-than-sanctified trash-talking with online opponents is the very "name" of the game: call of duty.

The game is based on the Allied nations answering the call to stand against the Axis powers in World War II. This was no minor insurgency against poorly equipped rebels armed with outdated muzzleloaders. This call was against the premier industrial and military powers of continental Europe and the Far East. Along with its cutting-edge military technology and blitzkrieg tactics, the German army struck fear into the hearts of the world. The deeply embedded samurai Bushido code and, as Dan Carlin puts it, "intensity" in Japanese culture shaped an Allied opponent who preferred suicide at one's own hand or collective banzai charges rather than facing capture.[1] They were no joke. These were just *some* of the opponents faced by farm boys, taxi drivers, school-teachers, and young men with forged birth certificates who answered the call of duty. It wasn't a video game or a virtual reality. It was real life. Everything had real-world implications. In the following section, I'd like to suggest a parallel to the Christian duty of giving a reasoned defense of the faith.

Duty Matters: The Christian Duty to Contend for the Truth

In his signature work *Reasonable Faith*, the great apologist William Lane Craig quotes J. Gresham Machen's ominous warning, "False ideas are the greatest obstacles to the reception of the Gospel. We may preach with all the fervor of a reformer and yet succeed only in winning a straggler here and there, if we permit the whole collective thought of the nation to be controlled by ideas which prevent Christianity from being regarded as anything more than a harmless delusion."[2] Notice *when* Machen made this observation: 1913. Even then, Machen saw where the long-term damaging effects of higher criticism of the Bible and Darwinian materialism would lead.[3] Craig concludes, "Unfortunately, Machen's warning went unheeded, and biblical Christianity retreated into the intellectual closet of Fundamentalism."[4] While there were pockets of Christian

---

1   Dan Carlin, "Supernova in the East I," July 14, 2018, in *Hardcore History*, podcast, MP3 audio, 4:28:17, https://podcasts.apple.com/ca/podcast/show-62-supernova-in-the-east-i/id173001861?i=1000415837465; editors of Encyclopaedia Britannica, "Seppuku," Britannica, last modified September 10, 2019, https://www.britannica.com/topic/seppuku.

2   J. Gresham Machen, "Christianity and Culture," *Princeton Theological Review* 11 (1913): 7; cited in William Lane Craig, *Reasonable Faith: Christian Truth and Apologetics*, 3rd ed. (Wheaton, IL: Crossway, 2008), 17.

3   See Archer's rebuttal of the JEPD theory that the Old Testament is little more than plagiarized Canaanite literature: Gleason L. Archer, *A Survey of Old Testament Introduction*, rev. ed. (Chicago: Moody, 2007), 71–153.

4   Craig, *Reasonable Faith*, 17.

leaders who took seriously the call to intellectually contend for the truth, on a macro level the Western church either opted for a cold deistic traditionalism or a shallow anti-intellectual emotionalism.

For example, in reaction to the famous Scopes Trial, Fundamentalists adopted the mantra "Read your Bible." Not surprisingly, the broader culture assumed that the Bible and science were mortal enemies. Many seminaries, whose task was to equip ministers and missionaries to be effective and faithful Christian leaders, capitulated to prevailing theories of their day that essentially gutted the gospel. The results were tragic. How could pastors preach the gospel with passion if their training undermined the veracity of the biblical text from which a sermon is supposed to come? How were missionaries to suffer persecution for the "good news" if such news was not accurate? You see, biblical passion and commitment are grounded in a confidence in the truth. Why study how to give a reasoned defense if the Christian worldview is full of holes? Nobody wants to buy a house sitting on a fault line. Even if you believe the tenets of historic Christianity, why bother with apologetics if reason and evidence play no significant role in Christian faith?

Craig's personal story bears witness to this decline. After earning his doctorate under Wolfhart Pannenberg, Craig accepted a full-time teaching position in philosophy of religion at an evangelical divinity school. There, after six years, he faced a potentially career-threatening set of circumstances that ultimately propelled him into the international spotlight. According to Craig, the dean of the seminary decided that "apologetics was no longer a useful discipline for the church."[5] Imagine having two earned European doctorates, being fluent in German and French, and having no employment.

Devastated by this unexpected blow, Craig reached such a point of financial desperation that he confesses, "I was reduced

---

5   William Lane Craig, "What Is the Meaning of Failure for the Christian?," sermon, Johnson Ferry Baptist Church, January 1, 2007, Marietta, GA, https://www.reasonablefaith.org/videos/lectures/what-is-the-meaning-of-failure-for-the-christian.

to calling churches in the yellow pages for support."[6] Nevertheless, Craig identifies this apparent tragedy as the catalyst that eventually led to the broadening of his influence. He states, "It was only by being kicked out of the little evangelical pond that we were catapulted into this broader world of scholarship and ministry that we have enjoyed since then and that we continue today through Reasonable Faith. It started because of a seeming disaster."[7] Being catapulted out of the evangelical world led Craig to the University of Louvain, where he completed postdoctoral work in divine foreknowledge and human freedom, as well as the theory of time. Decades later, contemporary Christianity is now enjoying a virtual renaissance of apologetics thanks to the labors of Craig, Alvin Plantinga, Gary Habermas, John Lennox, Paul Copan, and J. P. Moreland, just to name a few. The current apologetics movement resembles a return to the charge given to the early church, "contend for the faith" (Jude 3).

Why is there a moral duty for believers to explain the veracity of the Christian worldview? First, Christians have a responsibility to contend for the truth because of the gospel's eternal ramifications. By this, I mean we should have a deep sense of compassion for unbelievers. The Christian understanding of hell should produce this at a basic level. Maybe this is in part why the apostle Paul reminded the church at Corinth, "Therefore, knowing the fear of the Lord, we persuade others" (2 Cor. 5:11). Christianity is a missionary faith. The exclusivity of the Christian message calls for a precise and loving articulation of the gospel. Jesus sent his disciples into the world to make disciples of all nations (Matt. 28:19–20). If the gospel of Jesus is true, we have a moral responsibility to share it with others (1 Peter 3:15).

Second, Christians have a duty to contend for the truth because it glorifies God (1 Peter 3:15). The psalmist writes, "Ascribe to the

---

6   Craig, "What Is the Meaning of Failure?"
7   Kevin Harris and William Lane Craig, "Does God Slam Doors Shut?," October 19, 2009, in *Reasonable Faith Podcast*, MP3 audio, 21:08, https://www.reasonablefaith.org/media/reasonable-faith-podcast/does-god-slam-doors-shut.

Lord, O families of the peoples, ascribe to the Lord glory and strength! Ascribe to the Lord the glory due his name; bring an offering, and come into his courts! Worship the Lord in the splendor of holiness; tremble before him, all the earth!" (Ps. 96:7–9). A significant thread of the Christian gospel is the worthiness of God to receive obedience and worship.

Before going further, let me clarify that there's a vast categorical difference between God seeking his glory and us seeking our own. For example, consider the opening line of Rick Warren's *The Purpose Driven Life*, "It's not about you."[8] Most people would likely offer verbal agreement, even if their life choices say the opposite. If we were to dig into the thought, we'd probably hear something like this, "It's true that it's not about you, and if you think it is about you, then you have a problem." What is the problem? Why is it that we don't like being around self-consumed people? At the heart of it, it bothers us because deep down, we know it's morally inappropriate and irrational to live life like it's all about "me." The self-consumed person is living in a false reality.

It's easy to point this out in others. The ancient Babylonian king Nebuchadnezzar built a massive golden statue of himself and commanded everyone to worship it. This ranks high on the "yikes!" scale. God later disciplined Nebuchadnezzar to help him see that it wasn't about him (Dan. 4:28–37). The Communist North Korean government promotes the worship of its dictator Kim Jong Un.[9] Crazy, right? But how do I respond when a customer support representative is less than supportive or when an EGRP

---

8   See Rick Warren, *The Purpose Driven Life: What on Earth Am I Here For?*, exp. ed. (Grand Rapids: Zondervan, 2002), 21.

9   Jayant Bhandari reports, "North Korea is a perfect tyranny. . . . They have organized this tyranny in ways that were unimaginable to me, and people have been completely brainwashed. If this country goes through a real election today, I'm absolutely sure Kim Jong-un would win more than 99% of the votes without even trying to manipulate it. People are slaves in that country." Jonathan Roth, "North Koreans Are Literally Worshipping Kim Jong-un," Business Insider, July 3, 2017, https://www.businessinsider.com/north-koreans-worship-kim-jong-un-2017-7.

(extra-grace-required person) needs even more of my limited time? Again, it's a piece of cake to identify the "it's all about me" attitude in others, but it's super-easy to miss the log sticking out of my own eye (Matt. 7:1–6).

On the other hand, how do we make sense of the claim that it is all about the glory of God? Because it is! Far from megalomania, it is altogether right and proper for God to desire praise and glory because *he actually deserves it.* It's wrong for us to take the credit because we don't deserve it. The apostle Paul puts it this way, "For from him and through him and to him are all things. To him be glory forever. Amen" (Rom. 11:36). The word *glory* essentially "represents Hebrew *kabod* with the root idea of 'heaviness' and so of 'weight' or 'worthiness.'"[10] R. E. Nixon argues that God's glory is the most important concept in the Bible.[11] Defending the truth brings glory to God because it helps people understand who God really is and how he is worthy of their worship. As we will see, God's glory becomes magnificently clear in Jesus Christ.

Third, contending for the truth is quite simply obeying God's directive. Jesus teaches that loving God included the use of one's mind, "You shall love the Lord your God with all your heart and with all your soul and with all your mind. This is the great and first commandment. And a second is like it: You shall love your neighbor as yourself. On these two commandments depend all the Law and the Prophets" (Matt. 22:37–40). Loving God involves meeting others' practical needs (Matt. 25:35–40; James 2:14–17). But Jesus also includes properly *thinking* about God. Effectively contending

---

10 R. E. Nixon, "Glory," in *New Bible Dictionary,* eds. I. Howard Marshall, A. R. Millard, J. I. Packer, and D. J. Wiseman, 3rd ed. (Downers Grove, IL: Inter-Varsity, 1996), 414.

11 Nixon, "Glory," 414. Easton writes, "The phrase 'Give glory to God' (Josh. 7:19; Jer. 13:16) is a Hebrew idiom meaning, 'Confess your sins.' The words of the Jews to the blind man, 'Give God the praise' (John 9:24), are an adjuration to confess. They are equivalent to 'Give God the glory by speaking the truth.'" *Easton's Bible Dictionary* (New York: Harper & Brothers, 1893), 291.

for the truth requires loving God with the mind as well as the heart, although we have to be careful not to draw too stark a distinction between the two (Matt. 22:37). According to Jesus, we miss a crucial component of fulfilling the Great Commandment without it.

Some of us may be the first ones to serve a Thanksgiving meal at a homeless shelter or help a neighbor with a house project. We're all about serving and meeting practical needs. Others of us may have found schoolwork, reading, or big words downright intimidating. Francis Schaeffer provides some encouragement for those of us who find ourselves a bit timid to tackle the big questions and objections, "The ancients were afraid that if they went to the end of the earth they would fall off and be consumed by dragons. But once we understand that Christianity is true to what is there, true to the ultimate environment—the infinite, personal God who is really there—then our minds are freed. We can pursue any question and can be sure that we will not fall off the end of the earth."[12]

How can Schaeffer make such a claim? Because the Christian worldview gives us unrivaled resources to understand the complexities of the world. If the God of the Bible exists, then Christianity provides a helpful grasp not only of how the world came to be but also of the character of the one who brought it into existence. The Christian worldview is the key that frees the mind to properly function rather than wander aimlessly in the intellectual wilderness, grasping for threads of meaning in an uncaused universe with no ultimate point or purpose.

Schaeffer also recognizes the responsibility of contextualizing and communicating the Christian message to each successive generation, "Each generation of the church in each setting has the responsibility of communicating the gospel in understandable terms, considering the language and thought-forms of that setting."[13]

12 Francis A. Schaeffer, *The Complete Works of Francis Schaeffer: A Christian Worldview*, vol. 2, *A Christian View of the Bible as Truth*, 2nd ed. (Wheaton, IL: Crossway, 1985), 377.

13 Francis A. Schaeffer, *Escape from Reason* (Downers Grove, IL: InterVarsity, 1968), 120. John R. Franke reminds us, "No matter how persuasive,

Successfully contending for truth requires a working knowledge of the prevailing cultural narrative because apologetics is far from a static discipline.[14]

Why Apologize?

What do we mean by *apologetics*? The apostle Peter writes, "But in your hearts honor Christ the Lord as holy, always being prepared to make a defense to anyone who asks you for a reason for the hope that is in you; yet do it with gentleness and respect" (1 Peter 3:15). Peter's point is that Christians should prepare themselves to give a reasoned defense to those seeking answers.[15] The Greek word for "defense" is *apologia*; it serves as the root for our English word *apologetics*.[16]

Loving our neighbors well includes engaging in robust arguments in order to overturn false belief systems. We do this out of love for the person rather than to egotistically carve another notch in the belt while we listen to Drowning Pool's "Let the Bodies Hit the Floor." We could say that apologetics is the art of loving people

---

beautiful, or successful past theologies or confessions of faith may have been, the church is always faced with the task of confessing the faith in the context of the particular circumstances and challenges in which it is situated." *The Character of Theology: An Introduction to Its Nature, Task, and Purpose* (Grand Rapids: Baker Academic, 2005), 116.

14 Kevin Vanhoozer suggests that Christian wisdom is the real aim of evangelical theology ("The Voice and the Actor: A Dramatic Proposal about the Ministry and Minstrelsy of Theology," in Stackhouse, *Evangelical Futures*, 90). Similarly, Stanley Grenz defines the task of theology as "assist[ing] the people of God in hearing the Spirit's voice speaking through the text so that we can live as God's people—as inhabitants of God's eschatological world—in the present" ("Articulating the Christian Belief-Mosaic: Theological Method after the Demise of Foundationalism," in Stackhouse, *Evangelical Futures*, 125).

15 Thomas R. Schreiner, "1 Peter," in *CSB Apologetics Study Bible*, ed. Ted Cabal (Nashville: Holman, 2017), 1550.

16 Cf. Frederick William Danker, ed., *A Greek-English Lexicon of the New Testament and Other Early Christian Literature*, 3rd ed. (Chicago: University of Chicago Press, 2000), 117.

by addressing their questions in an intellectually rigorous yet gentle and respectful manner.

Think about it this way: Do you remember the last time you were at odds with another person, and suddenly you realized that you were mistaken? Horror of horrors! They were right and you were wrong. It's that one-liner, story, or "What about?" question that unlocked your mental vault. Immediately, it all came into focus and you realized just how far off base you actually were. Maybe it was a question of fact. Or you may have been blind to the fact that you were acting like a jerk. What can strongly affect our response is *how* the other person carries out the "mic drop" moment. Knowing that you're wrong is a tough road. Walking that road is even more challenging. But if the delivery comes with the additional items of snark, sarcasm, or spite, we will be more tempted to dig in, even when we *know* deep down that we're in the wrong. On the other hand, if the person's attitude exudes gentleness and respect, then we're far more likely to admit what we now realize is the truth.

When I was a teenager, I received a forwarded email. Yes, I had an email address in high school and actually used it. It was in the days of beepers, portable boom boxes, and crazy-expensive cell phones that weighed as much as an engine block. If you wanted to walk around with some tunes, you needed to be able to shoulder press at least 225 pounds. To own or talk on a cell phone, you needed an oil well in your front yard to pay for it. Good times! Anyway, this forwarded email carried "breaking news" that the famous atheist Madalyn Murray O'Hair had faked her death and was now leading a charge to ban all faith-oriented broadcasting. It sounded like something "Straight Outta Stalingrad." I was concerned and immediately forwarded it to several people. There was just one problem: it wasn't true. Even worse, it was a modified form of an older false rumor.[17]

---

17 John Dart, "Rumor of Atheist Airwave Attack Persists: Broadcasting: A False Rumor That Madalyn Murray O'Hair Is Petitioning the FCC to Ban All Religious Programming Is 15 Years Old," *Los Angeles Times*, April 14, 1990, https://www.latimes.com/archives/la-xpm-1990-04-14-ss-1129-story.html.

One of the guys who received my forwarded email didn't let it slide. He called me out on it like a Marine drill instructor finding a cadet cheating on pushups. He patronized my error of passing along unverified information by giving me something akin to a legal brief that demolished the points of the original message. Then he said I was naive and elaborated on what he perceived to be my cognitive limitations. Guess what? Even though his bedside manner left much to be desired, he was right! Even as I was reading his response, a sinking feeling began to grow in my heart. I knew I was wrong. Dead wrong. I had bought into a 1990s version of fake news and, worse, spread it to others as if it were true. However, because of his tone and tenor, I didn't *want* him to know that he had shown me the error of my ways. Maybe you've been there before. It's when you know they're right and you're wrong, but because their attitude just ticks you off, you don't want to give them the pleasure of knowing they won. Instead of an apology, you want to slap down a "Bye, Felicia!"

I share this story to illustrate the importance of *how* we deliver a reasoned defense of Christianity. Gentleness and respect effectively prepare the emotions and lower the tension so that the mind and volition can absorb compelling arguments for biblical Christianity. Indiscriminately dropping what we self-assuredly label as "truth bombs" without the accompanying spirit of gentleness and respect may get us a high view count on a YouTube clip or two. But it will be largely ineffective in making disciples. Apologetics is far more than dry data dumps, because humans are complex creatures. Yes, we're rational (or at least some of us are some of the time). But we also have these things called feelings. And our tone influences whether people really "hear" us or not.

Tone Matters Because People Matter

For us to love people well, we need to be exclusive in our theology but inclusive in our tone and personal skills. Here's what I mean: we never compromise on the clear teachings of Scripture. For example,

Christians believe that salvation is found only through Jesus Christ, who is the way, the truth, and the life (John 14:6). But we should do our utmost to be winsome, kind, and simply a nice person to be around. We should be willing to, from the heart, welcome every single person from *every* background and belief system, loving them regardless of where they come from or their current lifestyle. Genuine followers of Jesus have a deep conviction that every person has intrinsic value because they've been made in the image of God. Remember that in debates or one-on-one discussions, apologetics and the manner in which we communicate is like the bait of the gospel, and repentance from sin and faith in Jesus are the hook.[18]

Here are a couple of guardrails if you find yourself unintentionally steamrolling people rather than effectively making disciples. First, Christians are called to compassionately persuade non-Christians of the truth of the gospel. Second Corinthians 5:11 reads, "Therefore, knowing the fear of the Lord, we persuade others." God calls us to reach out to the struggling rather than strong-arm our neighbors into believing. Persuasiveness includes rigorously appealing to the mind with deep moral sentiments that reflect God's law engraved on the conscience (Rom. 2:14–16). There is no excuse for abrasive or underhanded tactics. Respect is the key here. Responding with a tempered disposition is a sign to others that you've at least graduated Maturity 101 and recognized that being a jerk isn't a spiritual gift.

We have all found ourselves losing respect for a person who shows a pattern of emotionally unhinged reactiveness. We may *like* certain people because they are funny, sing well, throw a football with precision, or have some other marketable skill that we find appealing. However, the people we *respect* and genuinely listen to are (or should be) those with character and integrity. I am not excluding entertainers or professional athletes from this category. In fact, the platform of fame can be a tremendous springboard for the advancement of the gospel.

---

18 Ray Comfort, "I Love Apologetics," Living Waters, February 5, 2018, https://www.livingwaters.com/i-love-apologetics.

Here's the point: if people do not respect our character, they will be less prone to be persuaded by our message. Notice how the apostle Paul connects influence within the church with both sound doctrine and strong personal character, "But as for you, teach what accords with sound doctrine. . . . Show yourself in all respects to be a model of good works, and in your teaching show integrity, dignity, and sound speech that cannot be condemned, so that an opponent may be put to shame, having nothing evil to say about us" (Titus 2:1, 7–8). The point is that for people to "hear" and not revile our sound doctrine, our integrity and dignity must be unassailable. Online or in-person invectives and abrasive rhetoric rarely lead others out of false belief systems.

Second, Jesus did not call us to pick fights or seek out controversial matters as gimmicks for self-centered notoriety. The apostle Paul reminds believers, "And the Lord's servant must not be quarrelsome but kind to everyone, able to teach, patiently enduring evil, correcting his opponents with gentleness. God may perhaps grant them repentance leading to a knowledge of the truth" (2 Tim. 2:24–25). Did you catch it? There it is again: gentleness. Notice how the text fuses rigorous intellectual reasoning and gentleness. This is fathoms apart from theological compromise. We are well within the bounds of orthodoxy to say that correcting *without gentleness* is blatant disobedience to Scripture. Remember to avoid the false dichotomy between doctrinal fidelity and a winsome way of interacting with others. Reason and evidence are incredibly important, but gentleness is how we emotionally prepare the other person to receive those reasons for following that evidence. Emotional preparation effectively precedes epistemological receptivity. Let us strive to be consistent: a people marked by truth, gentleness, and respect (1 Peter 3:15). Let us seek to be led by the Holy Spirit in exuding the strength of gentleness. Our attitude should show some evidence of the peace and fortitude Jesus Christ promises his followers.

Before we go further, let me, as a pastor and professor, acknowledge the shortcomings of some churches and Christians in treating all people well. The vast majority of professing Christians and Bible-believing churches I have personally been acquainted with genuinely desire to love people. It's just that some of us may not know precisely how. Either way, none of us bat at 100 percent. To be an effective witness for Jesus Christ, we need to realize that there is already a stereotype awaiting us, fashioned in the factory of post-rational contemporary Western culture. Let's look at a few common pitfalls.

Pitfall #1: The Church Curmudgeon

If you've never heard of the Church Curmudgeon Twitter handle (@ChrchCurmudgeon), prepare to be blessed. You don't need a heavily churched background to chuckle at this parody account, or even laugh so hard you snort like a seal. Think Mr. Wilson from *Dennis the Menace* meets grouchy church member. It's a mode of communication that is doctrinally accurate but emotionally abrasive. It's patting oneself on the back for "speaking or preaching the truth" but neglecting to explain the context or the backdrop of a biblical worldview. Such communication likely alienates those with little Bible background. People hear a gruff voice growling, "Get off my lawn!" For Bible-believing Christians, the issue has rarely been one of biblical fidelity, but rather of taking the time and effort to speak in an *articulate* yet biblical way. Articulate treatment is necessary when we handle sensitive and complex challenges. Otherwise, we just make a mess of it. Doctors, engineers, dentists, psychiatrists, and other professionals live in the real world of "precision or catastrophe," and Christians should seek to expand their toolkit to include scalpels and stitches rather than just a collection of sledgehammers.

Pitfall #2: The Compromising "Christian"

A second pitfall is that of the compromising "Christian." Why the quotation marks? Think about sports "greats": Mark McGwire,

Barry Bonds, Tonya Harding, Lance Armstrong, the Communist East German Olympic female swimming team from 1968 to 1980, and the list goes on.[19] Compromise creates a black eye on otherwise notable achievements. All Christians are faced with the temptation to compromise, but Christian leaders are increasingly coming under especially acute pressure. L. Russ Bush noted in 2001, "The challenge to divine authority is growing, and yet among Christians, a spirit of renewal is also growing. It is as if the wheat and the tares are nearing that anticipated final ripening stage, and a divine harvest is near. Intellectual leaders who guide the Christian community through these final days before the harvest must be able to discern the dangers of intellectual compromise. The church has greater spiritual power than all of her enemies combined, but compromise is her Achilles' heel."[20] Professing Christians who modify clear biblical teaching to fit their own emotional experiences (or sins) often view their new position as theologically enlightened. Thus, they accommodate rather than confront moral erosion. They downplay exclusivist language, cherry-pick Bible verses, and in so doing laud themselves for their so-called open-mindedness. In preaching, this attitude manifests itself by focusing almost exclusively on felt needs and ignoring robust theology at all costs. The Christian message then becomes just another self-help option that appeals primarily to the emotions rather than the intellect. It's candy for the emotions. It doesn't heal anything but tastes good for an hour a week, followed by a hard crash of reality.

In a misguided attempt to "love people," the medicine becomes diluted and exchanged for the temporary placebo effect of believing that "God loves you just as you are." Instead of asking the hard questions, Scripture becomes subservient to sentiment. An inquiry follows from this: Who is the real you? For Christians, our identity is

---

19 Todd Boldizsar, "The 40 Worst Cheaters in Sports History," Bleacher Report, December 9, 2010, https://bleacherreport.com/articles/537712-the-40-worst-cheaters-in-sports-history.

20 L. Russ Bush, *The Advancement: Keeping the Faith in an Evolutionary Age* (Nashville: Broadman & Holman, 2003), 5.

not in our sins but in our Savior. When we speak of love, we should ask, What is love? and most importantly, What is God's love? God's love confirms our value but confronts our sin. Max Lucado says it this way, "God loves you just the way you are, but he refuses to leave you that way. He wants you to be just like Jesus."[21] When church leaders allow fear and cultural trends to dictate the church's direction, the end result is that broken people seeking help are left with little more than sugar-coated one-liners, self-improvement tips, and no Redeemer. Instead of directing people to their need for a savior, compromised clergy trip over one another in a mad rush to christen the next culturally accepted sin. Rather than a faith in the God of the ages, whose grace is greater than sin, they're left with an anemic Jesus who doesn't actually save anybody because no one is sinful enough to need a savior. If you're clergy and you find yourself in this description, I encourage you to return to your first love.

Pitfall #3: Being Complicit and Silent

A third pitfall is to be silent and complicit. Consider this the polar opposite of the curmudgeon pitfall. Some Christians don't want to offend others, so they never speak up in a misguided attempt to be tolerant. But silence is not the same as tolerance. Neither does tolerance demand agreement. Forced conformity is tyranny. Tolerance is the willingness to rationally dialogue without resorting to physical violence or any other sort of coercion. Cancel culture is the polar opposite of tolerance. For Christians, there's *unity* in the gospel, but not a cultish conformity.

Equating disagreement and hate is a false dichotomy because disagreement and hate are not synonymous. We can disagree with others and still not hate them. If I'm being honest, I don't even agree with everything that I do. Think about it. All of us sometimes do or think things that we know we shouldn't. A consistent Christian says,

---

21 Max Lucado, *Just Like Jesus: A Heart Like His* (Nashville: Thomas Nelson, 2012), back cover.

"I love you too much not to speak up and to allow you to continue in a direction that I believe will harm you." Not to warn a person who is living in sin is a terribly unloving act.[22]

Instead, God calls Christians to speak with moral clarity, no matter how unpopular it may seem. Our approach should be molded by confidence in Jesus Christ and compassion toward all persons. Jesus himself provides the framework for acting with genuine compassion. Al Mohler writes, "We must not be silent where the Bible speaks. . . . Love requires us to tell the truth."[23] We should speak the truth in love, but we cannot fully love without speaking the truth.

At this juncture, I would like to appeal to those who disagree with the Christian message. How far are you willing to take your disagreement with Jesus Christ and his followers? Suppose you support shutting down or canceling opposing voices (religious institutions, Christian schools, Bible-believing churches, etc.) through litigation or public policy. In that case, you're setting yourself up for that same power to be used to shut down *your* voice if the pendulum of politics and power swings the other way. If we value freedom, we may strongly disagree with one another but still advocate for the liberty to express our respective viewpoints. Anything less becomes a less desirable circumstance in which to live.

Even if you are not a Christian, you should expect Christian leaders to be honest about what Scripture actually teaches and to do so in a way that captures the style, substance, and spirit of the text.[24] Concerning smooth-sounding but disingenuous sermons, in the words of Kimberly Wilkins, "Ain't nobody got time for that."

---

22 S. Donald Fortson III and Rollin G. Grams, *Unchanging Witness: The Consistent Christian Teaching on Homosexuality in Scripture and Tradition* (Nashville: B&H Academic, 2016), xii.

23 R. Albert Mohler, "My Take: The Bible Condemns a Lot, but Here's Why We Focus on Homosexuality," *CNN Belief Blog*, May 21, 2012, https://religion.blogs.cnn.com/2012/05/21/my-take-the-bible-condemns-a-lot-but-heres-why-we-focus-on-homosexuality.

24 Steven W. Smith, *Recapturing the Voice of God: Shaping Sermons Like Scripture* (Nashville: B&H Academic, 2015).

Tension is not a bad thing. Cults and cult leaders have no internal doctrinal tension. Everything is figured out. If we're willing to hear it out, press through, and allow God to speak to us through his Word, there's tremendous personal growth awaiting us on the other side. In physical exercise, it's often the workouts we want to avoid that have the greatest benefit (#LegDay).

Mark 1:14–15 states, "Jesus came into Galilee, proclaiming the gospel of God, and saying, 'The time is fulfilled, and the kingdom of God is at hand; repent and believe in the gospel.'" So to whom does Jesus's command to repent apply? Every single one of us. Can we agree that the gospel cuts all of us somewhere and in some way? There was never a class or group of persons to whom Jesus granted an exception clause on the command to repent. There are no people who need Jesus less than others. Romans 3:22–23 tells us, "For there is no distinction: for all have sinned and fall short of the glory of God." The gospel message is clear: we all need what none of us has—a transformed heart that allows us to love and follow God. That's why we all need Jesus. Saying yes to God requires saying no to yourself.[25] Jesus never lowers the cost (Luke 9:23–26).

In conclusion, should we even care about apologetics in the local church or as individual Christians? Absolutely! If people can operate businesses, teach in classrooms, administrate home lives, and operate million-dollar machinery, then they can handle robust apologetics. If you're a Christian, strive to improve your communication skills. Read more. Get up early or stay up a little later. Learn from critical thinkers to help increase your knowledge. Seek the Holy Spirit's help in your verbal and written defense of the gospel. Seek to be saturated by the love of God. Pray for your interaction with others to take the posture of Christ-glorifying humility. Deny yourself and exalt Christ. But never ever lower the high call of Jesus Christ. Go "reverse Nike" and just *don't* do it. Selling out is

---

25 See Sam Allberry, *Is God Anti-Gay?*, rev. and exp. ed. (London: Good Book Company, 2015).

a losing investment. Be faithful to communicate the good news of Jesus Christ, and let the chips fall where they may. Be courageous. Be teachable. Be humble. But never compromise on the core issues of the faith.

CHAPTER 2

LOVING PEOPLE WELL
WORLDVIEW PRESUPPOSITIONS

We've all heard it before: one size does *not* fit all. Different people process experiences and even data differently. If you are searching for a spiritual category for this chapter, you may consider biblical discernment as reason's sidekick for effective apologetics. As we've already mentioned in this book, the chief component of apologetics is loving God with all of one's mind by giving a reasoned defense to inquiring minds. When it comes down to the method or tactics of apologetics, we cannot overestimate the value of discernment with the aid of the Holy Spirit.

Here's what I'm getting at: to be maximally effective apologists, we must develop various approaches to meet a diverse set of personalities and connection points. Simply put, some people have an innate appetite for statistics and numbers-driven data. Some of us are "feelers." We feel the music, and heart-stirring stories move us. Our intuitions are deeply important to us.

Still others of us have no rhythm other than our overengineered calendars. Any basic personality test and even common experience reveals these sorts of indicators. Here's what I would encourage you to consider: No matter what area of apologetics interests *you*, remember that apologetics is not ultimately about you. Rather, it is to bring glory to God by giving a well-crafted set of arguments and rebuttals that are immersed in humility. The hope is that God will use your efforts to awaken the unbeliever. So if apologetics is not merely about scratching our own intellectual itches but about worshipping God and serving others, then let's eclectically extend our repertoire beyond a theological one-trick pony. Specialties are great (I wrote close to a three-hundred-page dissertation on a very specific topic), but narrow focus should not be at the expense of practical battlefield effectiveness.

Overview of Worldview Presuppositions

Before moving further, let's examine the power of *worldview presuppositions*. What on earth are they? If a worldview is the lens through which we see the world, then presuppositions are the granular data that form the foundation. Little tidbits of information gleaned from nightly newscasts, conclusions from a friend's experience of being mistreated, and a million other residual micromemories construct our deep-seated macroperspective. It's the entire collection of seemingly tiny conclusions and takeaways. Let's be honest: most of these are not critically assessed. Presuppositions are simply assumed. It would be safe to claim that a significant portion of our worldview presuppositions are absorbed rather than evaluated, and this is not necessarily a bad thing. As we will see, some things are properly basic, and we are well within reason to simply accept them as true.

So here's the point: if we are called to contend for the truth with broken people in a broken world, we need to know what we're working with. Apologetics handles arguments, but those arguments will fall flat more times than not *unless the worldview is challenged*. Sci-fi fans will remember the all-too-frequent defense shield technology that almost all alien spaceships seem to be equipped with. Until the shield is down, the force of the earthling missiles collapses harmlessly on the surface. The same goes for worldviews.

How do we challenge one's worldview? We must know, at least in some general sense, what sort of data underlies it. Consider this a kind of soil or strata sample. For example, suppose one holds to a naturalistic worldview (no God, no soul or spirit, and therefore, no miracles). In that case, there will always be in his or her own mind another way to explain away the evidence for the resurrection of Jesus of Nazareth.[1] The naturalistic worldview is a robust (but not insurmountable) blockade against opposing evidence. So what do we do with the evidence and arguments? We continue to deliver them. By all means, unleash the entire artillery battalion, but do not forget the sappers.[2] We do our work to chip away at the foundation of naturalism or any other "ism" contrary to the truth because, to take and hold ground, the battle includes both the mountain strongholds (the obvious) and the tunnels (the stuff lurking beneath the surface).

Granted, some belief systems take a lot of work to deconstruct. On a recent flight, I was seated next to a passionate defender of flat earth theory. After hearing his case, I responded, "I just haven't been able to get my mind around it." He didn't get it. What do you do in an age of disinformation and irrationality? Do what you can with what you have, and trust God to continue his work even with the little pebble you attempted to place in one's shoe.

The very first chapter of the apostle John's gospel contains a fascinating, unwarranted presupposition that Jesus quickly overturned, "The next day Jesus decided to go to Galilee. He found Philip and said to him, 'Follow me.' Now Philip was from Bethsaida, the city of Andrew and Peter. Philip found Nathanael and said to him, 'We have found him of whom Moses in the Law and also the prophets wrote, Jesus of Nazareth, the son of Joseph.' Nathanael said to him, 'Can anything good come out of Nazareth?' Philip said to him, 'Come and see'" (John 1:43–46).

Did you catch Nathanael's immediate response? We're not able to definitively discern his tone, but it couldn't have been all that neutral with a retort like that! He dismissed Jesus right out of the gate simply

---

1   Many thanks to my good friend Gary Habermas for routinely driving this point home. Gary R. Habermas, "Miracles," lecture, Liberty University, Lynchburg, VA, February 18–22, 2013.

2   Cf. Alexander Hamer, "Battles That Shaped History: Vienna," Real History, September 4, 2017, https://realhistory.co/2017/09/04/battle-of-vienna.

because of where Jesus was raised. Here's where it becomes even more interesting: Nathanael was from Cana, a tiny village in Galilee. Craig L. Blomberg comments on how Nathanael "used something of a double standard when he displayed prejudice toward insignificant Nazareth."[3] Maybe it was a general dismissal of people from humble beginnings or a projection of Nathanael's own insecurities. Or it could have been the all-too-common jealousy of those who feel small in their own eyes seeing someone like them achieving more than they have. Either way, notice how Philip does not respond with a heavy-handed guilt trip or throw his hands up in frustration and walk away. He simply says, "Come and see" (v. 46), which is what Jesus said to seekers, "Come and you will see" (v. 39). Nathanael's presupposition was as wrong as wrong could be, and I'm so thankful!

Sports is another area where presuppositions are glaringly evident. If you are a sports fan, you want the call to go your way. No coach, player, or fan is stoic during game time. I'm certainly not when the Dallas Cowboys play! (Sidenote: I've always said I'd like to have the Cowboys serve as the pallbearers at my funeral so they can let me down one last time. The struggle is real.) Think about it. We boo the referees when a close call goes to the other team. Then, if they miss our team's blatant penalty, we either try to ignore it or say that it equals out because of a poor call on the previous play. Here's my point: we are biased about far more than just sports. Again, that's not necessarily negative. We just need to be aware that apologetics involves more than premise one of the kalam cosmological argument or successfully splitting the horns of the Euthyphro dilemma.

The Power of Worldview Presuppositions

Let's dive into the power of worldview presuppositions. More than four hundred years before the birth of Christ, the renowned Athenian historian Thucydides observed, "The way that most men deal

3   Craig L. Blomberg, "John," in *CSB Apologetics Study Bible*, eds. Ted Cabal, et al. (Nashville: Holman Bible, 2017), 1308.

with traditions, even traditions of their own country, is to receive them all alike as they are delivered, without applying any critical test whatever."[4] Challenging accepted tradition is a dangerous and tricky business.[5]

So how does one tread through the minefield of longstanding worldview presuppositions? The first step is identifying them. Whether they realize it or not, Westerners are children of the Enlightenment and, regardless of how much they may fight against it, are almost predisposed to think of the world in naturalistic terms. It's their natural default. The Enlightenment's residual effects are one of the silent factors that often go unnoticed in the volleys fired over theology and philosophy. Even with the advances made in recent decades by Christian philosophers, many of the approved ideas in the wider professional philosophical community are still tainted by Enlightenment presuppositions. Any vestige of supernaturalism is dismissed a priori.[6]

---

4   Thucydides, *The History of the Peloponnesian War*, trans. Richard Crawley (Seattle: Amazon Digital Services, 2011), loc. 186 of 7940, Kindle.

5   Enthusiasm for moral clarity and virtue may be applauded in theory but rarely in application. Brave souls willing to shine the light of conscience on a culture's treasured traditions will likely find a similar welcoming as David Hume's "gloomy hair-brained enthusiast," who "after his death, may have a place in the calendar; but will scarcely ever be admitted, when alive, into intimacy and society, except by those who are as delirious and dismal as himself." David Hume, *An Enquiry concerning the Principles of Morals: Oxford Philosophical Texts*, ed. Tom L. Beauchamp (New York: Oxford University Press, 1998), 147.

6   John Hare points out the way ethicist Philip Kitcher's methodology systematically excludes from consideration certain religious convictions, assuming that they fail to make the threshold for conditional mutual engagement. Hare argues that this significantly detracts from the effectiveness and consistency of Kitcher's overall pragmatism. See John E. Hare, *God's Command* (New York: Oxford University Press, 2015), 292. Hare notes where Kitcher's arguments can be found: Philip Kitcher, *The Ethical Project* (Cambridge, MA: Harvard University Press, 2011); Kitcher, *Living with Darwin: Evolution, Design, and the Future of Faith* (New York: Oxford University Press, 2007), chap. 5; and Kitcher, *Life after Faith: The Case for Secular Humanism* (New Haven, CT: Yale University Press, 2014), chap. 1.

Grasping even a CliffsNotes-level understanding of the power of worldview presuppositions effectively peels back the layers of academic haze so that the elephant in the room becomes visible. All scholars have biases, and one could argue that the most biased are those claiming their studies are solely birthed out of a pristine, Platonic quest for truth. Nobody is as blind to biases as those who think they have none. Michael R. Licona remarks, "One's bias is not only difficult to overcome but is often difficult to recognize."[7] May God grant us self-awareness! Cutting-edge research suggests that many leading atheists of the past did not arrive at their atheism through an intellectual search for the truth but from a combination of deep emotional scarring or an entrenched pattern of sordid depravity.[8] Craig Keener takes a more aggressive approach when he argues that "rationalism and empiricism often presented themselves as throwing off an older epistemology of revelatory authority, yet these systems demand (by authority) an a priori acceptance of their own epistemologies. Put more simply: everyone has presuppositions. Those who dismiss others' evidence because those offering it have different presuppositions are being neither charitable nor open-minded, and they short-circuit the possibility of dialogue."[9] Perhaps this is in part Luke Timothy Johnson's point when he writes, "For Modernity, belief in a creed is a sign of intellectual failure. Creeds involve faith, and faith makes statements about reality that can't be tested."[10] Could it be that a great deal of resistance to Christianity is presuppositional rather than a thoughtful but firm rejection of biblical claims? At this stage, we should be careful not to imply that a denial of Christianity is *always* the result of gross

---

7   Michael R. Licona, *The Resurrection of Jesus: A New Historiographical Approach* (Downers Grove, IL: IVP Academic, 2010), 59.

8   James Spiegel, *The Making of an Atheist: How Immorality Leads to Unbelief* (Chicago: Moody, 2010), 105–6.

9   Craig S. Keener, *Miracles: The Credibility of the New Testament Accounts* (Grand Rapids: Baker Academic, 2011), 1:199.

10 Luke Timothy Johnson, *The Creed: What Christians Believe and Why It Matters* (New York: Doubleday, 2005), 2.

moral sin. Still, it's entirely possible that a refusal to accept the moral implications of the risen Jesus is not exclusively intellectual.[11]

For example, consider the categorical presuppositions of naturalism. If miracles are possible, one can make the argument that what can be known is not always contained within the parameters of strict, natural laws. Since the Enlightenment, the West's overwhelming presupposition is that the universe is a closed system rendering miracles categorically impossible. The influence of David Hume, possibly the most influential philosopher on miracles and religious epistemology, is considered to have nailed the proverbial nail into the coffin of the possibility of miracles (e.g., the resurrection of Jesus). The following statement captures the fulcrum of his understanding of what we can know and how we can be sure, "If we take in our hand any volume; of divinity or school metaphysics, for instance; let us ask, Does it contain any abstract reasoning concerning quantity or number? No. Does it contain any experimental reasoning concerning matter of fact and existence? No. Commit it then to the flames: for it can contain nothing but sophistry and illusion."[12] Semantics aside, Hume's gaping fallacy is rather apparent: he attempts to reject theology, metaphysics, and any other nonempirical disciplines via a philosophical statement! Hume makes his argument in philosophical terminology, not mathematical or scientific formulas. He slips into the all-too-common trap of "(logical) rules for thee, but not for me."

Although this book's scope will not allow for a full-scale response to Hume, it would be a disservice to the discussion if there were no mention of Craig Keener's shattering rebuttal. In a devastating 1,172-page critique of Hume's antisupernaturalism, Keener gives not only a powerful undercutting defeater, but also provides

---

11 James K. Beilby notes, "The reasons for unbelief [in the Christian message] are incredibly diverse, and many of these reasons are hidden deep under psychological and personal baggage." *Thinking about Christian Apologetics: What It Is and Why We Do It* (Downers Grove, IL: IVP Academic, 2011), 25.

12 David Hume, *Hume's Enquiries Concerning the Human Understanding and Concerning the Principles of Morals* (New York: MacMillan, 1897), 165.

an unprecedented academic treatise on the topic of miracles. Keener
argues that Hume's argument against miracles is problematic:[13] "He
argues from nature's uniformity against miracles, which is the point
in question. He generalizes from the alleged lack of good testimony
for miracles to exclude what may in fact be good testimony for
miracles. . . . If Hume argues that no evidence in principle can be
sufficient to compel belief in miracles, his claim might succeed to
the extent that the evaluator of the evidence held tenaciously to
antimiraculous presuppositions, but is not logically necessary if the
evaluator is genuinely open-minded on the question."[14]

Essentially, Keener charges Hume with playing with loaded dice.
The card deck has been surreptitiously marked. Hume's epistemological standards forego an open investigation of the evidence and
commit the age-old fallacy of begging the question (*petitio prin-
cipii*, "assuming the initial point"). Furthermore, Hume's appeal to
"'uniform experience' involved passive recollection of a sequence
of events known to oneself and possibly one's colleagues, and no
more."[15] Twenty-first-century levels of international interaction
dwarf Hume's geographical and cultural isolation as a Scottish
scholar in the eighteenth century. Keener's exploitation of the gap in
Hume's armor is both fair and needed because it illustrates the fallacy of making absolutist judgments based on limited information.

Again, a presupposition is simply an unproven assumption,
something that is imported to the writing table or science lab that
affects the conclusions drawn. I am not saying that presuppositions
cannot be warranted but rather that they do not appear in an argument's visible structure. One must dive beneath the surface to
investigate the pylons that hold the rig up. No one gets a free pass
in the area of presuppositions.

Diplomatic immunity serves the purpose of international di-
plomacy, but exemption from rationality quickly stifles dialogue.

---

13   Keener, *Miracles*, 1:143.
14   Keener, *Miracles*, 1:143.
15   Keener, *Miracles*, 1:147–48.

Such exemption is on display when a person assumes that they are correct because they hold a prestigious degree or sit in a position of power. Professors are guilty of this fallacy when they exclusively appeal to their own authority. Unless you're into the divine right of kings, it becomes a little bizarre when mortals believe they are above the laws of logic and reason. Although pure objectivity is likely unattainable, persuasive apologists must highlight the recurring need to clear out the intellectual cobwebs.[16]

Let me be clear: I am not arguing against presuppositions or strong beliefs. To do so would be awkwardly inconsistent. Rather, I'm arguing that claims of pure neutrality may be a red flag for an attempted agenda cover-up. Feigned neutrality, with a driving campaign to exclude all data that does not neatly fit into a preestablished agenda, holds great potential for hampering real dialogue and research.[17] Phillip E. Johnson's point on materialistic Darwinism is quite relevant here: "The last subject I should address before beginning is my personal religious outlook, because readers are bound to wonder and because I do not exempt myself from the general rule that bias must be acknowledged and examined. . . . My purpose is to examine the scientific evidence on its own terms, being careful to distinguish the evidence itself from any religious or philosophical bias that might distort our interpretation of that evidence. . . . The question I want to investigate is whether Darwinism is based upon a fair assessment of the scientific evidence or whether it is another kind of fundamentalism."[18] Here, Johnson undercuts the charge of those who assume they have the corner on the market of purely analytical thinking. The question is not whether one has

---

16 As C. Fred Smith observes, "We often assume the truth of our own worldview without carefully examining it." *Developing a Biblical Worldview: Seeing Things God's Way* (Nashville: B&H Academic, 2015), 2.

17 On the Christian position, Augustine laments, "I fear my own self-deception, for my corrupt heart lies even to itself." *The Confessions of St. Augustine: Modern English Version* (Grand Rapids: Spire, 2008), 19.

18 Phillip E. Johnson, *Darwin on Trial* (Downers Grove, IL: IVP Books, 1993), 9–10.

presuppositions, but whether one's presuppositions are sound. Not all presuppositions are equally warranted.[19] All sides must play by the same set of epistemological and rational rules for genuine discussion to exist at all.

Authority and Worldview Presuppositions

So let's take a brief breather. What if you unloaded even portions of what we've examined thus far, maybe to a non-Christian friend over coffee or during a public speaking course at a secular university? If you're waiting for heavily secularized twenty-first-century crowds to enthusiastically chant your name for espousing historic Christian truths, don't hold your breath. Then again, they may chant your name, but it likely won't be to cheer you on. It may sound more like, "Off with your head!" Or, "Let's cancel your social media platform, remove your tax-exempt status, or deny your tenure track professorship." Part of persuasive apologetics is being alert to foreseeable objections. In the following section, I'll walk you through some ways to respond to pushback without getting embroiled in unproductive minutiae. The following colloquialism applies both to farming and apologetics, "Your job is to grow corn. In order to grow corn, sometimes you have to get down in the weeds. But don't stay in the weeds, because your job is to grow corn." Let's take a look at how to deal with the weeds so that we can bear genuine fruit, to the glory of God. Imagine the following objections and rebuttals.

OBJECTION:　　It sounds like you're trying to advocate those outdated, traditional moral standards. We're in the twenty-first century now. You need to be on the right side of history. Christians need to catch up with the times!

19　Daniel Mitchell wisely notes, "Bullheadedness in holding to one specific scientific hypothesis is not science; it's politics." "Science in Apologetics," lecture, Liberty University, Lynchburg, VA, October 23, 2012.

REBUTTAL 1:   Consistent Christians want to be on the right side of God and stick with him, whose truth and character do not change.[20] The early church was told the same thing, but that's precisely why they *changed* history. They were unwilling to depart from what made Christianity Christian.[21]

REBUTTAL 2:   To say that a current viewpoint is definitively and absolutely going to be on the right side of history shows that one really doesn't know history. It may also indicate a fair amount of arrogance that one in fact knows what is the "one" viewpoint that is on the "right side" of history. It sounds, at best, a bit presumptive. Throughout the ages, what was often accepted as standard (and even moral) has gone from the spotlight to the dumpster of public opinion. One day you're Vanilla Ice with your one hit, and the next, you're out in the cold on the ice.

REBUTTAL 3:   Ultimately, this entire discussion comes down to a question of authority: Who decides who needs to change? Are we willing to allow God's Word to speak, or are we committed to twisting it to say what we want it to say (or to ignoring it altogether)? If you disagree with the Bible, what qualifies you to revise it? I'm not trying to be smart-alecky here. It's a fair question to ask: What more extraordinary sagacity do you possess that warrants overturning the cumulative ancient wisdom of Scripture? If God exists, then he is a maximally Great Being and holds

---

20   See Charles H. Spurgeon, "The Immutability of God," sermon, New Park Street Chapel, January 7, 1855, https://www.spurgeon.org/resource-library/sermons/the-immutability-of-god/#flipbook.

21   Nancy R. Pearcey, *Love Thy Body: Answering Hard Questions about Life and Sexuality* (Grand Rapids: Baker Books, 2018), 188.

authority that we do not. Every time we attempt to override or toss away God's design, we find ourselves grinding against the very fabric of the universe.

OBJECTION: But I feel constricted by Christian morality!

REBUTTAL: Our sinful flesh *does* box us in, in one way or another, but the good news of Jesus Christ offers a way out. The apostle Paul, while sharing his testimony with King Agrippa, recounts, "And when we had all fallen to the ground, I heard a voice saying to me in the Hebrew language, 'Saul, Saul, why are you persecuting me? It is hard for you to kick against the goads.' And I said, 'Who are you, Lord?' And the Lord said, 'I am Jesus whom you are persecuting'" (Acts 26:14–15). Goads were prods to keep animals out of ditches and pointed in the right direction. "The Lord" in this story is Jesus, and his point to Paul (then Saul) is evident, "Turn to me instead of pushing against me."

To gain a better vantage point on the issue of authority, let's take a brief look at one of the most prominent New Testament scholars of the twentieth century, German Lutheran scholar Rudolf Bultmann (1884–1976). Bultmann desperately wanted Christianity to survive the modern scientific era. He wondered, How relevant is a religion with miracles like walking on water and raising the dead in such an era, with its nuclear fission and intergalactic spacecraft? Christianity needed to adapt to the culture and keep up with the times. He led the charge with the proposed solution of "demythologizing" not only the New Testament but also the entire corpus of Christianity. How so? By removing "false" stumbling blocks, like references to anything supernatural. You know: Jesus healing people, casting out demons, raising the dead, walking on water, controlling the weather, etc. Basically, the essential elements that make Christianity the supernatural revelation that it is. Bultmann makes his case:

The purpose of demythologizing is not to make religion more acceptable to modern man by trimming the traditional Biblical texts, but to make clearer to modern man what the Christian faith is. He must be confronted with the issue of decision, be provoked to decision by the fact that the stumbling-block to faith, the *skandalon*, is peculiarly disturbing to man in general, not only to modern man (modern man being only one species of man). Therefore, my attempt to demythologize begins, true enough, by clearing away the false stumbling-blocks created for modern man by the fact that his world-view is determined by science.[22]

Bultmann's aim to make Christianity palatable to modern man is encapsulated in quite possibly his most famous statement, "It is impossible to use electric light and the wireless and to avail ourselves of modern medical and surgical discoveries, and at the same time to believe in the New Testament world of spirits and miracles."[23] In other words, historic Christianity and science are incompatible. So if there is an apparent conflict, who gets the boot? For Bultmann, a supernatural Christianity must be adjusted to fit the prevailing presuppositions.

In his own words, Bultmann sought to deliver Christianity from itself. The real question is one of authority, and it bubbles up to the surface throughout Bultmann's arguments. But why should Christianity be compelled to make concessions to fit the needs of another worldview? As Kevin Vanhoozer explains, "In the self-assured world of modernity, people seek to make sense of

---

22 Rudolph Bultmann, *Kerygma and Myth: A Theological Debate*, eds. Austen Farrer and Hans Werner Bartsch (London: Society for Promoting Christian Knowledge, 1953), 2:182–83.

23 Rudolf Bultmann, *New Testament and Mythology, and Other Basic Writings*, ed. and trans. Schubert M. Ogden (Philadelphia: Fortress, 1984), 4; quoted in Alvin Plantinga, *Where the Conflict Really Lies: Science, Religion, and Naturalism* (New York: Oxford University Press, 2011), loc. 1100 of 6220.

the Scriptures, instead of hoping, with the aid of the Scriptures, to make some sense of themselves."[24] Bultmann failed to recognize that his nonsupernatural worldview is both intellectually problematic and exclusive of the broader community of humanity. Any scientist worth his or her salt will readily agree that scientific hypotheses are continually shifting.

By attempting to demythologize Christianity and thus remove barriers to its acceptance, Bultmann did the exact opposite. Keener notes, "Bultmann, however, unwittingly excluded from the modern world the majority of the world's population . . . in a manner that current sensitivities would regard as inexcusably ethnocentric. . . . *Bultmann's perspective was not a result of biblical scholarship per se but of a particular philosophic epistemology.*"[25] In other words, outside the West, most cultures have no problem with the supernatural. By trying to "save" Christianity by carving out the miraculous, Bultmann created a tragic barrier between Scripture and the world's majority population.

Thankfully, many today are realizing the shortcomings of naturalism. Theologians are not the only ones leading the shift away from this crumbling edifice. David Brooks writes,

> The atheism debate is a textbook example of how a scientific revolution can change public culture. Just as *The Origin of Species* reshaped social thinking, just as Einstein's theory of relativity affected art, so the revolution in neuroscience is having an effect on how people see the world. . . . Over the past several years, the momentum has shifted away from hard-core materialism. The brain seems less like a cold machine. It does not operate like a computer. Instead, meaning, belief and consciousness seem to emerge mysteriously from idiosyncratic

---

24 Kevin J. Vanhoozer, *The Drama of Doctrine: A Canonical Linguistic Approach to Christian Theology* (Louisville: Westminster John Knox, 2005), 20.
25 Keener, *Miracles*, 1:8 (emphasis mine).

networks of neural firings. Those squishy things called emotions play a gigantic role in all forms of thinking. Love is vital to brain development.[26]

Walter Wink levels a stinging indictment for CINO (Christian in name only) compromisers when he writes, "People with an attenuated sense of what is possible will bring that conviction to the Bible and diminish it by the poverty of their own experience."[27] Bultmann's error was fundamentally explaining away the miraculous reality woven throughout all of Scripture. Bultmann's approach has devastated entire denominations that have adopted his so-called enlightened view of the Bible.[28]

Again, the question here is, Why does God's Word need to be adjusted to fit a stylish current worldview? Why should the Ancient of Days become subservient to a fleeting shadow? What a waste to exchange the one life we have to impact the world for temporary cultural popularity. To throw into the wood chipper the testimony of Christian martyrs, Scripture, and what makes Christianity Christian is to wake up a generation later and find that you're left with nothing. Make no mistake: the cultural craze of today will drop you like a bad habit tomorrow. Sometimes revolutionaries become victims of their own revolution.[29] Whether Caesar's Roman Empire,

26 David Brooks, "The Neural Buddhists," *New York Times*, May 13, 2008, http://www.nytimes.com/2008/05/13/opinion/13brooks.html.

27 Walter Wink, "Write What You See: An Odyssey," *Fourth R*, May/June 1994, 6.

28 Joe Carter, "FactChecker: Are All Christian Denominations in Decline?," Gospel Coalition, March 17, 2015, https://www.thegospelcoalition.org/article/factchecker-are-all-christian-denominations-in-decline. Also see David Haskell, "Liberal Churches Are Dying. But Conservative Churches Are Thriving," *Washington Post*, January 4, 2017, https://www.washingtonpost.com/posteverything/wp/2017/01/04/liberal-churches-are-dying-but-conservative-churches-are-thriving.

29 Leon Trotsky is a fitting but tragic example. An early leader in Russia's Communist Bolshevik Revolution, Trotsky later became a *persona non grata* of Soviet totalitarianism and was assassinated via an axe attack in Mexico City in 1940 by order of Josef Stalin. Skepticism is always warranted in cases of those pursuing unmitigated power in the name of doing good.

Marx's almighty State, ISIS's caliphate, Narendra Modi's Hindu nationalism, or Western clergy who say God's clear call to repent is no longer relevant, all of this will eventually crumble into the ever-growing dust pile of vain attempts to fire God and establish a new authority over human existence. Jesus Christ still lives, and his church will move forward with the good news of the gospel. Trying to save Christianity from itself does just the opposite.[30]

Here's where the philosophical category of worldview presuppositions becomes intensely personal. It's the question we can answer only for ourselves: Are you genuinely willing to consider God's perspective? Are you willing to consider that God's plan is good or even best? Think about it: if I'm genuinely not convinced something is best for me, I'm not going to follow it. One of the aspects of the image of God is that we all desire to live fulfilling lives. Tragically, some even take their own lives in the quest for happiness because they think death is preferable to life. Before deciding to reject what may seem unfamiliar or confrontational, we all would do well to assess whether we're willing to entertain a different perspective before flatly rejecting it. Manfred Brauch's question should cause us to give serious consideration, "What if God really does exist and has a view by which he will judge the world in the end?"[31] Worldview presuppositions comprise far more than smart-sounding rhetorical icing on the analytical cake. Rather, they shape the tone and trajectory of our life and, if God in fact does exist and Jesus rose from the dead, our eternity as well.

---

30 Mark Tooley, "Mystery of Liberal Church Decline," Stream, July 11, 2018, https://stream.org/mystery-liberal-church-decline.
31 Walter C. Kaiser Jr., Peter H. Davids, F. F. Bruce, and Manfred T. Brauch, *Hard Sayings of the Bible* (Downers Grove, IL: IVP Academic, 1996), 543.

APOLOGETIC TACTICS

Bernard and Fawn M. Brodie humorously recount, "James I of England was later to say ironically that armor provided double protection—first it kept a knight from being injured, and second, it kept him from injuring anybody else."[1] For us to be effective apologists, our methods must not be cumbersome. Think Jackie Chan—quick, versatile, and devastatingly effective, with a dash of humor for good measure. Let's talk about the tools available to the apologist. Beyond a grasp of basic theology, I suggest that the most effective tool is philosophy. Yes, you read that correctly—*philosophy*. But don't be alarmed! It doesn't mean you have to use million-dollar words at the drive-through, increase your bifocal game, wear bow ties, or spend Saturdays at the library. Think of philosophy as helping us think well. In fact, philosophy was historically known as the "handmaiden of theology."[2] William Lane Craig goes as far as to say, "I

---

1   Bernard Brodie and Fawn M. Brodie, *From Crossbow to H-Bomb: The Evolution of the Weapons and Tactics of Warfare* (Bloomington: Indiana University Press, 1973), 37.

2   L. Russ Bush warns, "No good theology can ignore philosophical implications, nor can philosophy ignore theological considerations." "The Rest of the Story: A Bibliographical Essay on Apologetic Writing in the Nineteenth and Twentieth Centuries," in *Classical Readings in Christian Apologetics, A.D. 100–1800*, ed. L. Russ Bush (Grand Rapids: Academie Books, 1983), 385.

believe that today the Christian seeking after truth will probably learn more about the attributes and nature of God from works of Christian philosophers than from those of Christian theologians."[3] Let me be clear: I am not devaluing work in other disciplines. Undergraduate philosophy majors are often susceptible to this temptation, sort of like the way plebe guitar students view mastery of the four guitar chords in the key of G. At first blush, it gives a deceptive air of confidence over the uninitiated. The goal is not philosophical dialogue for its own sake, but to lead persons to Christ through the means of thinking well.

Contrary to what some of us have been told, theology and apologetics are intensely practical.[4] According to Francis Schaeffer, a Christianity divorced from real-life issues is no Christianity at all because "truth carries with it confrontation. Truth demands confrontation; loving confrontation, but confrontation nevertheless."[5] He's right. Contending for the truth necessitates knowing and articulating it. This will (hopefully) set the tone for the topic of apologetic tactics. That being said, apologetic approaches should be servants, not masters.

An Overview of Apologetic Tactics

Before going further, I'll provide a very brief overview of apologetic approaches. But first, let me share my first experience with this subject. I'll never forget it. During my first semester at Bible college, a guy wearing JNCO jeans and sporting a flat cap approached me in the computer lab. "I heard you like apol-

---

3   William Lane Craig, *The Only Wise God: The Compatibility of Divine Foreknowledge and Human Freedom* (1987; reprint, Eugene, OR: Wipf and Stock, 1999), 11.

4   Francis A. Schaeffer, *The New Super Spirituality* (Downers Grove, IL: InterVarsity, 1976), 29–30.

5   Francis A. Schaeffer, *The Complete Works of Francis Schaeffer: A Christian Worldview*, vol. 4, *A Christian View of the Church*, 2nd ed. (Wheaton, IL: Crossway, 1985), 110.

ogetics." It was a small school and I guess word traveled quickly. "Absolutely, bro. How about you?" I responded. He replied, "Oh, definitely." Then he dropped a bomb on me, "What apologetic methodology do you prefer?" I thought, *Apologetic what?* I thought apologetics was giving people reasons why Christianity is true. I had no clue that there were different methodologies. Although I was unaware of what he was talking about at the time, I'll be forever grateful for that conversation. This guy was super-smart and introduced me to various schools of thought, along with his preferred approach. So if you're unfamiliar with apologetic methodology, approaches, or tactics, take heart! We'll do a brief flyover of apologetic tactics and how we can form an effective and eclectic approach. So here we go!

Fideism

Several years ago, a young man who was raised in a legalistic background began attending our church. He devoured biblical content like a powerlifter at a Golden Corral buffet. This guy truly wanted to *know* the foundations of a Christian worldview. Having been raised in the church, he had this unshakeable drive to investigate what he had always been taught so that his faith could truly become his own. He was far from "that guy." You know the guy—the one who interrupts your small group with questions laced with fancy words, likes to argue with church leaders over minutia, and carries around an aura that says, "I'm smarter and more spiritual than you. Christian leaders before me didn't know a thing. I'm like Neo from *The Matrix*—'I am the one.' Because of my extensive theological vault acquired through reading blogs, you should be honored to be in my presence." If you haven't met *that* guy, just be sure you're not him.

By contrast, this guy showed a high aptitude for truth, accompanied with a humble spirit. He expressed a specific desire to study apologetics, so we gave him a copy of Douglas Groothuis's *Christian Apologetics: A Comprehensive Case for Biblical*

Faith.[6] His father found out and was less than enthused. Instead of considering how many Christian parents would be delighted for their young adult to show an interest in learning more about God, he scolded his son, "We shouldn't need books like that. Our faith is in Jesus, not in all this stuff. Philosophy? Not in this house!" It's still tough to believe this was the reaction of a professing Christian parent. The father then banned the young man from attending our church any further.

Here's the reason for sharing this story: whether the father realized it or not, he was thinking like a fideist. Groothuis defines *fideism* as "an attempt to protect Christian faith against the assaults of reason by means of intellectual insulation and isolation."[7] Fideism is essentially an anti-intellectual view of Christianity. It views reason and evidence with suspicion or outright antagonism. The brilliant and bearded Adam Lickey puts it this way, "Fideism accepts a path of blind faith to knowledge without the need to verify truth. To elevate faith above revelation is to ignore the God given faculties to comprehend truth from its source. God has given reason as a beautiful tool to use, in its proper epistemological place, to understand what God has said in and through His creation."[8] Fideism also shows itself in a lack of financial planning, organizational strategy, and wise living in general. It's the "all we need is faith" or "you have logic, I have faith" mindset, which is a dangerous misunderstanding of what faith actually is. We may even go as far as to call it the "Jesus juke" method.[9]

6   Douglas Groothuis, *Christian Apologetics: A Comprehensive Case for Biblical Faith*, 2nd ed. (Downers Grove, IL: IVP Academic, 2022).
7   Groothuis, *Christian Apologetics*, 60.
8   Adam L. Lickey, "Carl F. H. Henry's Presuppositional Theology and Its Implications within Educational Settings" (PhD diss., John W. Rawlings School of Divinity, 2019), 81, https://digitalcommons.liberty.edu/cgi/viewcontent.cgi?article=3105&context=doctoral. Lickey interacts with Norman Geisler's treatment of Søren Kierkegaard's thought. See Norman L. Geisler, *Baker Encyclopedia of Christian Apologetics* (Grand Rapids: Baker Books, 1999), 407.
9   Jon Acuff, "The Jesus Juke," *Stuff Christians Like* (blog), November 16, 2010, https://stuffchristianslike.net/2010/11/16/the-jesus-juke.

The Classical Method

Classical apologetics is a form of evidential apologetics but slightly differs from evidentialism in the fact that it's a two-step approach. First, you argue for God's existence by using general revelation (moral, cosmological, and fine-tuning arguments, etc.).[10] Second, you establish God's identity through special revelation—namely, the resurrection, historicity of Jesus, etc. In boxing terminology, arguments for God's existence are the jab, and the case for the resurrection is the knockout punch.

One angle of the first step is the debate over science and theology. The classical apologist says it's a false dichotomy to argue that science and theology are diametrically opposed to each other. Richard Dawkins and others from the "not so new now atheists" camp claim that Christianity is the mortal enemy of science. One can make a strong case that it was actually Judeo-Christian monotheism that provided the intellectual framework for the very notion of scientific thought. Rodney Stark writes,

> What the great figures involved in the sixteenth- and seventeenth-century blossoming of science—including Descartes, Galileo, Newton, and Kepler—did confess was their absolute faith in a creator God, whose work incorporated rational rules awaiting discovery.
>
> The rise of science was not an extension of classical learning. It was the natural outgrowth of Christian doctrine: nature exists because it was created by God. In order to love and honor God, it is necessary to fully appreciate the wonders of his handiwork. Because God is perfect, his handiwork functions in accord with *immutable principles*. By the full use of our God-given powers of reason and observation, it ought to be possible to discover these principles.

---

10 For an excellent resource on the various arguments for the existence of God, see Groothuis, *Christian Apologetics*, 161–609.

These were the crucial ideas that explain why science arose in Christian Europe and nowhere else.[11]

In other words, without a Christian framework that espoused a God of order, science would have had no grounding point in a world thought to be governed by magic spells, river spirits, mysticism, and outright witchcraft.

The Disney animated film *Moana* subtly illustrates this worldview in the song "You're Welcome." The demigod Maui is played by Dwayne ("The Rock") Johnson, who sings about being able to control the natural order. These lines are descriptive of a worldview without a God of reason and order who has created an ordered creation with predictable natural laws. Belief in miracles is not mysticism. Demigods, naiads, dryads, and other mystical beings "just messing around" are a far cry from an all-powerful creator God who may choose to temporarily suspend physical laws in order to work a miracle for his specific purposes, which flow from his perfect nature and attributes. Kenneth Samples comments, "Because the world is not divine and therefore not a proper object of worship, it can be an object of rational study."[12] Far from impeding scientific research, biblical Christianity, with its vast penchant for exploring and learning about God's creation, is a close friend of science. Thus, we have the two-step approach in classical apologetics.

Evidentialism

While both evidential and classical apologetics appeal to the common ground of evidence available to Christians and non-Christians,[13] the beauty of classical apologetics is the magnitude of its

---

11 Rodney Stark, *The Victory of Reason: How Christianity Led to Freedom, Capitalism, and Western Success* (New York: Random House, 2005), 22–23.

12 Kenneth Richard Samples, *Without a Doubt: Answering the 20 Toughest Faith Questions* (Grand Rapids: Baker Books, 2004), 193.

13 The *Stanford Encyclopedia of Philosophy* reads, "Contemporary epistemology of religion may conveniently be treated as a debate over whether *eviden-*

comprehensive approach (first the existence of God, then the identity of that God). Just to reiterate, classical apologetics leads us to theism, but not necessarily Christian theism. The classical arguments lead us to the existence of a maximally Great Being, but we lack clarity on the character and nature of that being.

Evidentialism digs into historical evidence that is available to everyone but that is also connected to the core of the Christian message. In my estimation, while classical apologetics is comprehensive and elaborate, evidential apologetics, in some cases, may help us get closer quicker to not only the existence of God but also the identity of the God that exists. The efficiency of evidential apologetics and its accessibility are well illustrated in the minimal-facts argument for the resurrection of Jesus. The minimal facts in this argument are important because they are accepted by virtually all critical scholars, Christian and non-Christian alike. They are as follows: (1) the death of Jesus via crucifixion; (2) the disciples' experiences, which they believed included appearances of the risen Jesus; (3) the early proclamation of Jesus's resurrection; (4) the transformation of the disciples, such that they were willing to die specifically for their belief in the resurrection; (5) Paul's conversion experience, which he also believed included an appearance of the risen Jesus; and (6) James's conversion experience, which he too believed included a similar appearance.[14] Evidentialism's power is found in leveraging evidence accepted by and available to all persons regardless of their philosophical or religious assumptions. Technically speaking, these historical evidences do not *prove* Jesus's resurrection. Instead,

---

tialism applies to religious beliefs, or whether we should instead adopt a more permissive epistemology. Here evidentialism is the initially plausible position that a belief is justified only if 'it is proportioned to the evidence.'" Peter Forrest, "The Epistemology of Religion," *Stanford Encyclopedia of Philosophy*, last modified June 22, 2021, http://plato.stanford.edu/entries/religion-epistemology.

14   Gary R. Habermas, *Philosophy of History, Miracles, and the Resurrection of Jesus*, 3rd ed. (Sagamore Beach, MA: Academx, 2012), 72. Also, see Habermas, *The Historical Jesus: Ancient Evidence for the Life of Christ* (Joplin, MO: College Press, 1996).

the force of the argument centers on what is the most reasonable explanation of the data. Outside of elaborate but futile attempts to explain away the empty tomb, we're left with either a miracle or a random freak accident.

In my view, I believe there are good reasons to think that the resurrection of Jesus is far from a bizarre occurrence. Rather, it occurs within the framework of the Hebrew prophets and their prophecies. Jesus even predicted his own death and resurrection (Matt. 16:21; 17:22; Mark 8:31; Luke 13:33). Without proper context, an event like the resurrection would be beyond mysterious—like "Syfy Channel comes to life on Friday the thirteenth" sort of freaky. But if the event dovetails *with* the rich tapestry of Scripture regarding the Messiah, the resurrection of Jesus can serve as a bridge to not only the existence of God but also the identity of that God. If you're interested in digging more into this topic and navigating around the potholes, or if you suspect that I am guilty of "special pleading," check out Habermas's work *The Risen Jesus and Future Hope*.[15] Habermas gives reasons to believe why this is more than just an incredible event—indeed, an event connected to the God of the universe.

Presuppositionalism

Presuppositionalism is a large tent, but a unifying definition could be "a school of apologetics influenced by Reformed Christianity that rejects the tools of classical apologetics."[16] It's essentially a denial of the relevance and efficacy of evidences. Here's the way it works: the effects of sin on the human mind are so extensive that a two-step, one-step, or any-step approach is insufficient to bring a person to faith in Christ. We all presuppose certain things that we cannot prove. For instance, we presuppose things like our own

---

15   Gary R. Habermas, *The Risen Jesus and Future Hope* (New York: Rowman & Littlefield, 2003), 53–88.
16   Groothuis, *Christian Apologetics*, 62.

existence, that communication is indeed possible, or that the chair you are sitting on (if you are sitting) will hold you up. If not, you would not be sitting in the chair.[17] In like manner, why can't the Christian presuppose the internally coherent Christian worldview? Rather than an offensive attack like the cosmological argument for the existence of God or the minimal-facts case for the resurrection of Jesus, presuppositionalism's power is different. It calls out non-Christians who naively assume that their own presuppositions get a free pass and that Christians bear the burden of proving their worldview is true.[18]

Several years ago, I had the opportunity to speak on apologetics in a formerly Communist European country. In a breakout leadership session, I presented the moral argument for the existence of God along with other standard apologetics content. I began noticing furrowed brows and raised eyebrows. At one point, a man raised his hand and inquired, "But if a person is unregenerate, can they even understand these sorts of arguments?" Then I realized what I was standing in: this particular group had been steeped in an extreme form of presuppositionalism (even though it had not yet been exposed to the term) and thought that argumentation and evidence were useless and even counterproductive in evangelism and apologetics. Because of human depravity, it was a waste of time to exercise arguments for God, Christ's exclusivity, and the veracity of Scripture, as well as any other logic-laden attempt to demonstrate the God of Scripture as real. My full response is in the section on the noetic effects of sin further in this chapter. Still, the short of it was this, "Why did you ask me to lead an apologetics conference if your version of apologetics doesn't include the heart of

---

17 Matthew J. Coombe, "Utilizing Presuppositional Apologetics for the Purposes of Formulating Theological Method, lecture, Liberty Baptist Theological Seminary, Lynchburg, VA, April 12, 2012.

18 However, the danger, in my estimation, is overestimating the noetic effects of sin. I will deal with this in detail in a later section of this book, hopefully graciously critiquing a version of presuppositionalism that takes the noetic effects of sin a bit too far.

apologetics—giving a reasoned defense of the faith? There seems to be a categorical confusion here: depravity or human fallenness does not mean the conscience and intellect are completely dismantled."

Let me be clear: I believe in the sovereignty of God. Without that, we edit Scripture and are left without a guarantee of hope or justice. However, the God who is sovereign is also the God who has ordained the use of means. One of those means is rigorously and persuasively arguing for *why* Christianity is true. Throughout this book, I advocate utilizing every available tool and approach as fitting to the audience or individual, to the glory of God.

Reformed Epistemology

What in the world is *Reformed epistemology*? Even saying it feels like your IQ jumps up a point or two. (I'll be calling it RE from now on.) RE is a close cousin of presuppositionalism. Fair warning: RE is complex stuff. No way around it. But let not your hearts be troubled! There are accessible tools in RE available to those of us who are not tempted to pull away for a weekend and plow through a philosophical monograph on modal logic. You can't talk about Reformed epistemology without mentioning Alvin Plantinga, whose "key philosophical move . . . is to argue that belief in God and the entire Christian worldview is one kind of belief that may be properly basic."[19] We're talking about the powerful tool of properly basic beliefs. In other words, you don't need an argument to be rationally justified for believing in God because properly basic beliefs do not *require* an argument. We'll take a more in-depth look at the unique power of RE in the next section.

Eclectic Apologetics

Eclectic apologetics is essentially the point of the first part of the book title. To persuasively answer tough questions, we must be versatile.

---

19 Groothuis, *Christian Apologetics*, 65.

Apologetics isn't a standardized assembly line. It's a battle within the mind, will, and emotions of actual people. And people happen to be messy, including you and me. We'll need different tactics at certain times. That's what eclectic apologetics is all about. In some cases, you'll do well to lead with presuppositionalism and RE. These can take away the opponent's ability to strike first by preempting their claim that "Christianity is unreasonable or irrational" and questioning their ability to reason on a naturalistic worldview. In other cases, the moral argument for God's existence could deeply stir someone who is troubled by human rights abuses in the world. It's not an issue of being a "Come at me, bro" smarty-pants but one of loving God by loving people well. One size does not fit all.

The Subtle Power of Reformed Epistemology

A brief excursus on RE will provide some helpful insight into a main ingredient of eclectic apologetics. Reformed epistemologist Kelly James Clark writes, "Belief in God, like belief in other persons, does not require the support of evidence or argument in order for it to be rational."[20] This simple form of indirect reasoning finds its roots in the writings of renowned philosopher Alvin Plantinga. Plantinga is credited with sparking a full-scale revolution within the philosophical community, leading to a resurrection of theism in academia. In the 1970s, the era of big shirt collars and even bigger hair, Plantinga's little book, *God, Freedom, and Evil*, lodged more scintillating questions than definitive answers.[21] When the dust settled, it became apparent to all but the most hardened partisans that the logical problem of evil was no longer a defeater against theism.

RE's central argument is that theism is exempt from the evidential requirement. Why? *Because theism is a properly basic belief.*

---

20 Kelly James Clark, "Reformed Epistemology Apologetics," in *Five Views on Apologetics*, ed. Steven B. Cowan (Grand Rapids: Zondervan, 2000), 267.
21 Alvin Plantinga, *God, Freedom, and Evil* (Grand Rapids: Eerdmans, 1974), 33.

What is a properly basic belief, and what are its criteria? Plantinga explains, "Theistic belief as produced by the *sensus divinitatis* is basic. It is also *properly* basic, and that in at least two senses. On the one hand, a belief can be properly basic for a person in the sense that it is indeed basic for him (he doesn't accept it on the evidential basis of other propositions) and, furthermore, he is *justified* in holding it in the basic way: he is within his epistemic rights, is not irresponsible, is violating no epistemic or other duties in holding that belief in that way."[22]

The distinction between reasonableness and absolute proofs is significant. Just because we may be unable to definitively *prove* our belief in God does not entail that Christianity or even mere theism is unreasonable. A more equitable question should be, "What is reasonable?" not "What is exhaustively provable?" In philosophy, proofs are about as common as hen's teeth, so the shift from absolute proofs to reasonableness drastically reframes the debate.

Ever since the Enlightenment, theists have primarily carried the burden of proof. Keener argues, "for miracles . . . Hume presupposes a standard of proof so high that any evidence is effectively ruled out in advance."[23] Principally unattainable proofs unreasonably replaced reasonableness. Plantinga identifies two kinds of objections emanating from the Enlightenment: (1) de facto objections, or arguments against the factuality of God's existence, and (2) de jure objections, or claims "that Christian belief, whether or not true, is at any rate unjustifiable, or rationally unjustified, or irrational, or not intellectually respectable, or contrary to sound morality, or without sufficient evidence, or in some other way rationally unacceptable, not up to snuff from an intellectual point of view."[24]

---

22 Alvin Plantinga, *Warranted Christian Belief* (New York: Oxford University Press, 2000), 177–78.

23 Craig S. Keener, *Miracles: The Credibility of the New Testament Accounts* (Grand Rapids: Baker Academic, 2011), 1:155.

24 Plantinga, *Warranted Christian Belief*, ix. Where perception is often reality, Plantinga simply sidesteps high-collateral de facto attacks, primarily addressed through evidential arguments, and focuses on de jure presuppositions.

A confessional advocate of the classical method, William Lane Craig applied a section from the RE playbook in his debate with atheist Frank Zindler in the summer of 1993. Craig so exposed Zindler's atheistic bias that the debate became somewhat humorous because of Zindler's unceasing and arbitrary demands for evidence. Craig posited a succinct form of Plantinga's suggestion to the degree that Zindler's purely evidential attack was dismantled to the point of embarrassment.[25] Zindler repeatedly pressed the issue of evolution. Craig then undercut Zindler's entire premise. For the sake of argument, the odds of evolution occurring are so statistically improbable that they are literally in the realm of miracles. If miracles happen, then God exists. Therefore, Zindler's argument about evolution proves, rather than disproves, God's existence (my paraphrase). To be clear, Craig never affirmed materialistic Darwinism but used Zindler's own assertions to undercut his entire worldview. In the words of Tom Haverford and Donna Meagle from *Parks and Rec*, "Treat yo'self," and go watch the debate.

This undercutting approach is useful in academic debates. But it's also applicable in everyday apologetics, even when the luxury of uninterrupted dialogue is often rare, especially with the electronic leash (otherwise known as the smartphone) that most of us carry. Instead of establishing a comprehensive argument *for* the existence of God, the goal of RE is to put a rock in one's shoe.[26] RE seeks to question entrenched a priori assumptions instead of enticing others into a toe-to-toe slugfest over who has the most evidence. On the responsibility of the burden of proof, Koukl argues, "Whoever makes the claim bears the burden. The key here is not to allow yourself to be thrust into a defensive position when the other person is making the claim. It's not your duty

---

25 *The Great Debate: Atheism vs. Christianity*, featuring William Lane Craig and Frank Zindler (1993; Grand Rapids: Zondervan, 1994), VHS.

26 Gregory Koukl, *Tactics: A Game Plan for Discussing Your Christian Convictions* (Grand Rapids: Zondervan, 2009), 46. Koukl's "Columbo tactic" does not wear Plantinga's label, but it conforms with RE's starting point.

to prove him wrong. It's his duty to prove his view."[27] Allowing non-Christians to carry their logic to its ending point eventually exposes unwarranted presuppositions.

When pressed for intellectual justification for his belief in God, Plantinga responds by asking why an argument is even required for warranted belief.[28] When one requires sufficient evidence for certain beliefs to be reasonable, Plantinga asks for specifics.[29] Again, why shouldn't theism be a properly basic belief? From here, the naturalist needs to give specific refutations as to why belief in God is not warranted outside of a probabilistic evidential argument. The theist is no longer automatically confined to the questioning stand in the courtroom of evidence, nor is the atheist allowed to assume the role of prosecutor. Plantinga's austere form of argumentation opens the door for the possibility of dialogue because it gives no preferential treatment to naturalistic assumptions. Naturalism cannot bear the weight of its own ultimatums.[30]

There is a whole slew of things that we cannot *prove* but that we all base our decisions on. These include the beliefs that there are minds other than our own,[31] that the universe was not created yesterday, that torturing children is morally wrong, and that *Die Hard* is indeed a Christmas movie.[32] You get the point. The high-sounding "I'm a rational person and only believe in what can be proven" is exposed for the intellectual facade that it is. Clark muses, "Reasoning must start somewhere. There have to be some truths that we can just accept and reason from. Why not start

---

27   Koukl, *Tactics*, 59.
28   Alvin Plantinga, interview by Robert Lawrence Kuhn, *Closer to Truth*, PBS, February 27, 2011, https://www.youtube.com/watch?v=NCscorlkYeU.
29   "The *de jure* rebuke is pretty vague and general." Plantinga, *Warranted Christian Belief*, 167.
30   Clark, "Reformed Epistemology Apologetics," 269.
31   Is it solipsistic in here, or is it just me?
32   See *What Is the Evidence for/against the Existence of God?*, moderated by William F. Buckley Jr., featuring William Lane Craig and Peter Atkins (1998; Norcross, GA: Ravi Zacharias International Ministries, 2006), DVD.

with belief in God?"[33] If you haven't yet added RE's undercutting power to your apologetics toolkit, I encourage you to consider it. It's a potent tactic to throw an overly confident skeptic off balance with the weight of his or her own claims.

Making confident claims based upon unwarranted assumptions is one of the least competent ways to use one's mind. As a case in point, Plantinga argues that atheism is a sign of improperly functioning rational faculties, rather than a sensible and evidenced conclusion.[34] The atheist naturally rebuts by questioning whether any assumption can qualify as a properly basic belief. Could properly basic beliefs be akin to an extreme form of epistemological fideism?[35] Plantinga anticipates a possible objection that any type of presupposition is warranted, "To recognize that *some* kinds of belief are properly basic with respect to warrant doesn't for a moment commit one to thinking all *other* kinds are."[36] It does not follow that because *some* properly basic beliefs exist, all beliefs are therefore warranted.

One weakness of RE is its lack of a strong, positive apologetic. Its strength of undercutting opposing claims carries with it a lessened emphasis on establishing positive reasons for believing in God. Plantinga argues that evidences are unnecessary for theism to be warranted, although he does give a list of two dozen or so theistic arguments.[37] Every tool has its function, and RE's

---

33 Clark, "Reformed Epistemology Apologetics," 270–71.

34 Plantinga, *Warranted Christian Belief*, 489–90.

35 This is the position that claims reason is unnecessary or counterproductive to belief. Richard Amesbury, "Fideism," Stanford Encyclopedia of Philosophy, last modified February 5, 2022, https://plato.stanford.edu/entries/fideism/#1.

36 Plantinga, *Warranted Christian Belief*, 334.

37 Alvin Plantinga, "Appendix: Two Dozen (or so) Theistic Arguments," in *Alvin Plantinga*, ed. Deane-Peter Baker (New York: Cambridge University Press, 2007), 203–27. Plantinga writes, "I've been arguing that theistic belief does not (in general) *need* argument either for deontological justification or for positive epistemic status (or for Foley rationality or Alstonian justification); belief in God is properly basic. But it doesn't follow, of course, that there aren't any good arguments. Are there some? At least a couple of dozen or so" (210).

is to probe and check worldview presuppositions. RE views evidential arguments as supplements, not staples, which logically stems from the premise that theism is a properly basic belief. Plantinga qualifies his list of arguments, "These arguments are not coercive in the sense that every person is obliged to accept their premises on pain of irrationality. Maybe just that some or many sensible people do accept their premises (oneself). What are these arguments like, and what role do they play? They are probabilistic, either with respect to the premises or with respect to the connection between the premises and conclusion, or both. They can serve to bolster and confirm ('helps' à la John Calvin), perhaps to convince."[38] Therefore, RE does not oppose positive arguments for theism, but at the same time, it does not consider such arguments necessary for a justified Christian belief. As American humorist Seba Smith's pre–politically correct adage goes, "There is more than one way to skin a cat."

RE is qualitatively unique in its approach. It can help us develop a high level of intellectual awareness to not take the naturalistic bait so prevalent in the current culture. Christian apologists from various theological backgrounds would do well to learn Plantinga's method of first assessing the foundations of claims before directly answering their assertions. In chapter 4, we'll take a more in-depth look at this under the objection "Faith is irrational; believing in God is checking your brain at the door." But for now, think of it as answering a question with a question. Why do theists or Christians automatically carry the burden to "prove" the existence of God? Who says proof is even a reasonable standard? Do not feel pressured to hand over the high ground without an argument. Don't acquiesce to others' ungrounded assumptions by immediately answering their questions at face value. Do not allow atheists to assume the role of prosecutor. Be like the Spartans at Thermopylae and the Texans at the Alamo: *Molōn labe*—"Come and take [it]!"

---

38 Plantinga, "Appendix," 210.

Gentleness and respect do not require giving in when you should stand firm. Be polite, gracious, and emulate Jesus's methodology—not in the sense of trying to discern another person's thoughts (that can be dangerous), but in not being pinned down by spurious questions. Jesus was the perfect example of respect and gentleness, yet he still routinely exposed faulty logic and groundless arguments.

So what is the proper role of reason in this eclectic apologetic approach? Daniel Kennedy recounts the example of the great Thomas Aquinas (1225–1274):

> His extraordinary patience and fairness in dealing with erring philosophers, his approbation of all that was true in their writings, his gentleness in condemning what was false, his clear-sightedness in pointing out the direction to true knowledge in all its branches, his aptness and accuracy in expressing the truth—these qualities mark him as a great master not only for the thirteenth century, but for all times. . . . Were St. Thomas living today he would gladly adopt and use all the facts made known by recent scientific and historical investigations, but he would carefully weigh all evidence offered in favour of the facts. Positive theology is more necessary in our days than it was in the thirteenth century.[39]

Here's the point: if all truth is God's truth, then use everything at your disposal. Reason, however, must not be confused with pure rationalism. Norman Geisler differentiates rationalists as those who try to *determine* all truth through reason, whereas Christians apply

---

39 Daniel Kennedy, "St. Thomas Aquinas," New Advent, accessed December 28, 2022, https://www.newadvent.org/cathen/14663b.htm. Aristotle's emphasis on reason significantly influenced Aquinas, as is evidenced by Aquinas dubbing Aristotle "the Philosopher." See Ralph McInerny, *St. Thomas Aquinas* (Boston: Twayne, 1977), 30–74.

reason to *discover* truth.[40] Reason is a tool, not a talisman. When understood in this light, the use of reason in apologetics provides a considerable amount of flexibility because probability, not certainty, is the criteria of sound argumentation.[41]

Eclectic Apologetics and Mixed Martial Arts

Apologetic methodologies vary as widely as approaches to self-defense and martial arts. RE displays incredible takedown power, but there's a noticeable lack of offensive weaponry. On the other hand, the classical apologist brings an astonishing array of offensive tools. Then there's the evidentialist who utilizes accessible historical data that provides a backdoor connection to a biblical framework.

All these methods have their respective strengths, and I believe we should use them regardless of our particular theological tribes. Whether you have a John Calvin motivational poster hanging in your room or say that *Free Willy* is your favorite movie just so you have an excuse to talk about free will, I would encourage you to be committed to the gospel rather than a particular apologetic approach. I'm not advocating theological compromise; rather, I'm suggesting we use every available tool within the tent of biblical Christianity.

Christians should resist the temptation to view their conversations as merely talking points or illustrations of a particular apologetic approach's superiority. The glory of God is our ultimate target in

---

40 Geisler, *Baker Encyclopedia of Christian Apologetics*, 428.
41 While outside the lines of evidential apologetics, Plantinga's work in RE has significantly advanced the viability of properly basic beliefs. Undercutting logical positivism, Plantinga argues that to require absolute proofs for beliefs is absurd. Why? Rational human decisions are made on the premise of reasonableness rather than absolute certainty. If this holds true, Plantinga has successfully defended theism as having a rightful place within the category of properly basic beliefs. Taken together with the classical wedge strategy, one need not attempt to prove the existence of God. One needs only to demonstrate that it is more reasonable to believe in God than not. See Plantinga, *Warranted Christian Belief*, 342–51. Plantinga also provides a scintillating defense against the "son of a great pumpkin" objection.

apologetics, so we aim at the practical targets of strengthening Christians and helping those far from God come to know God. Intellectual laziness or bullheaded methodological dogmatism may say more about our pride than about our commitment to the truth. Francis Schaeffer says it well regarding apologetic tactics and methodologies, "I do not believe there is any one apologetic which meets the needs of all people. And, as I said in the text of *The God Who Is There*, I did not (and do not) mean that what I wrote in that book . . . should ever be applied mechanically as a set formula. There is no set formula that meets everyone's need, and if only applied as a mechanical formula, I doubt if it really meets anyone's need—short of an act of God's mercy."[42] What a statement! While Schaeffer leaned toward presuppositionalism, he didn't methodologically restrict himself. His warning against a "mechanical formula" reminds us that persons are not automatons. Perhaps his actual experience of stepping beyond academic discussion and peer-reviewed publications to conversing with spiritually parched students broadened his horizons. It's one thing to read books about fishing. It's quite another to go out on the water and bait your own hook.

In what sense am I using the qualifier *eclectic*? The rising sport of mixed martial arts provides a relevant illustration. Bruce Lee, the only man to ever defeat Chuck Norris on screen (and widely acknowledged as the forefather of mixed martial arts), was famous for advocating the development of all aspects of one's fighting preparedness. One student of Lee recounts, "I found his training methods fascinating. His methods changed with every lesson he taught. They weren't structured—always spontaneous and improvisational."[43] In what has come to be known as "The Lost Interview" on the *Pierre Berton Show* in 1971, Lee was asked about his views on training for full-contact fighting. He responded. "Real fighting? Well then, baby, you'd better

42 Francis A. Schaeffer, *The Complete Works of Francis A. Schaeffer: A Christian Worldview*, vol. 1, *A Christian View of Philosophy and Culture*, 2nd ed. (Wheaton, IL: Crossway Books, 1982), 176.

43 Bruce Thomas, *Bruce Lee Fighting Words* (Berkeley, CA: North Atlantic Books, 2003), 106.

train every part of your body."[44] A fight could take the shape of a stand-up kickboxing match or go to the ground like a schoolyard brawl. Therefore, fighters may have developed a particular strength, but in order to survive, they need to adopt other skills because of the uncertainty of a fight's direction. Likewise, apologists may develop special strengths but must routinely add new skills and refresh old ones to be maximally persuasive due to the smorgasbord of worldviews.

To defend this metaphor, remember that the New Testament refers to related disciplines on a number of occasions. The apostle Paul compares the Christian life to a full-scale battle (Eph. 6:10–20) and encourages Christians to "fight the good fight" (1 Tim. 1:18) and "fight the good fight of faith" (6:12). He also alludes to the brutal Greek practice of boxing to illustrate self-discipline (1 Cor. 9:26). Then there's the Divine Warrior of Revelation 1 and 19, whose battle-hardened exploits are hardly G-rated or, in the catchphrase common on contemporary Christian radio, "safe for the whole family."[45] Thus, one may legitimately appreciate the correlation to mixed martial arts. Martial artists who limit themselves to one specific discipline, whether wrestling, jujitsu, boxing, or Barney Fife's study of karate through mail, will be ill-prepared in a real fight.

Intellectual Smokescreens: The Noetic Effects of Sin

Why do smart people choose crazy? I'm not talking about the Darwin Awards, Jeff Foxworthy's "Here's Your Sign" montage,

---

44 Bruce Lee, interview by Pierre Berton, *The Pierre Berton Show*, December 9, 1971, https://www.imdb.com/title/tt0767205.

45 The imagery of Revelation 19 is so spectacular it is difficult to come to a conclusion that the rider of the white horse represents anything other than deity. Eyes like blazing fire (19:12), wearing many crowns (19:12), name being synonymous with the word of God (19:13) (thus elevating him above simply a conduit of God's word), leads the armies of heaven (19:14), strikes down and rules the nations as the unrivaled sovereign (19:15), executes the wrath of God in a direct sense (19:15), and single-handedly defeat the beast, the kings of the earth, and their amassed armies, by executing judgment on them and delivering them over to the lake of fire (19:19–20).

YouTube's FailArmy videos from the mid-2000s, or interviews with the average person on the street that reveal a terrifying lack of basic historical knowledge. I'm referring to a willful ignorance of the truth about God. Intellectual smokescreens are when a person does not *want* to see. Unbelief is rarely *just* an intellectual issue. In this section, we will examine what philosophers and theologians refer to as the noetic effects of sin.

Noetic comes from the Greek word *nous*, which means "mind" or "intellect."[46] The idea is that sin has affected not only the cosmos but also how we process and think about the world. Sin has tainted our reason. No apologist is more prominent on this issue than Cornelius Van Til. Before going further, let me be clear: I greatly respect Van Til's commitment to the gospel and the glory of God. My critique on a particular aspect of his philosophy does not mean that we cannot learn much from him.

Van Til believes the noetic effects of sin are so extensive that "man is blind with respect to the truth wherever the truth appears."[47] The *imago Dei* has been irrevocably scrapped. If the noetic effects of sin are this extensive, then appealing to evidence through the use of reason is an exercise in futility.[48] Outside of a move of the Holy Spirit, a person's reasoning ability is totally flawed and, as far as apologetics is concerned, useless.[49]

However, the apostle Paul's description of unbelievers in Romans 1–2 seems to suggest otherwise. If unregenerate persons are

---

46   Frederick William Danker, ed., *A Greek-English Lexicon of the New Testament and Other Early Christian Literature*, 3rd ed. (Chicago: University of Chicago Press, 2000), 680.

47   Cornelius Van Til, *Christian Apologetics*, ed. William Edgar (Phillipsburg, NJ: Presbyterian & Reformed, 1976), 92.

48   Van Til, *Christian Apologetics*, 4.

49   Van Til quotes Calvin, "There is great repugnance between the organic movements and the rational part of the soul. As if reason also were not at variance with herself, and her counsels sometimes conflicting with each other like hostile armies. But since this disorder results from the deprivation of nature, it is erroneous to infer that there are two souls, because the faculties do not accord harmoniously as they ought." *Christian Apologetics*, 4.

without any epistemic access to God, then Paul's reference to the external witness of God's existence in nature is confusing. But just because non-Christians may *reject* the knowledge of God, it does not follow that they have no ability to *reason* about God. Furthermore, if natural theology is of no use, then why does Paul use it? J. P. Moreland provides some helpful commentary here, "I am not suggesting that the only thing in Scripture relevant to evangelism is rational argument and apologetics. However, I am suggesting that *apologetics is an absolutely essential ingredient to biblical evangelism*. And it is easy to see why. An emphasis on reasoning in evangelism makes the truthfulness of the gospel the main issue, not the self-interested 'fulfillment' of the listener."[50] Paul recognizes the external witness of nature not only to God's existence but also to the conscience as the innate witness to God's essential attributes (Rom. 1:18–21). Romans 2:14–15 reads, "For when Gentiles, who do not have the law, by nature do what the law requires, they are a law to themselves, even though they do not have the law. They show that the work of the law is written on their hearts, while their conscience also bears witness, and their conflicting thoughts accuse or even excuse them." Whatever the extent of the noetic effects of sin, it cannot mean the absence of a divine witness, a lack of knowledge of one's own moral guilt, or the inability to reason about God's attributes.

Romans 1–2 entails that unbelievers have intellectual access to both God's existence and his moral attributes.[51] According to Paul's anthropology, persons are sinners by nature and choice and can by no means justify themselves apart from Christ. Yet they still have

---

50 J. P. Moreland, *Love Your God with All Your Mind: The Role of Reason in the Life of the Soul* (Colorado Springs: NavPress, 1997), 132.
51 Kenneth D. Boa and Robert M. Bowman Jr. write, "This [human fallenness] does not mean that non-Christians know nothing about God. Augustine cited Romans 1:20 to show that some philosophers, especially Platonists, have been able from the creation to recognize the fact of a Creator God." *Faith Has Its Reasons: Integrative Approaches to Defending the Christian Faith*, 2nd ed. (Downers Grove, IL: Biblica Books, 2005), 16.

the internal barometer of God's law inscribed on the heart (Rom. 1:18–21; 2:14–16). John Calvin goes as far as to acknowledge, "Men of sound judgment will always be sure that a sense of divinity which can never be effaced is engraved upon men's minds. Indeed, the perversity of the impious, who though they struggle furiously are unable to extricate themselves from the fear of God, is abundant testimony that this conviction, namely, that there is some God, is naturally inborn in all, and is fixed deep within, as it were in the very marrow."[52] I believe that persuasive apologetics eventually appeals to the human conscience. The moral law of God is the apologist's internal ally regardless of what a person claims to believe about moral absolutes or even the existence of God. We see Paul's pattern of first appealing to the reason of non-Christians as a pathway to petition the conscience. Paul used the common ground of theism with the Athenians—albeit polytheism—to make an inroad for the resurrection (Acts 17:22–31). He "reasoned about righteousness and self-control and the coming judgment" with Felix to the point that the ruler became "alarmed" (24:25). Talk about speaking truth to power! Paul's approach is comparable to mixed-martial-arts apologetics in that he adapts to different audiences. Yet he still presses the truth of the resurrection, the necessity of repentance from sin, and the need for faith in Christ.[53]

On the other hand, Van Til's apologetic approach denies human reason the capacity that classicists and evidentialists ascribe to it.[54]

---

52 John Calvin, *Institutes of the Christian Religion*, ed. John T. McNeill, trans. Ford Lewis Battles (Philadelphia: Westminster, 1960), 45–46. See James Spiegel, *The Making of an Atheist: How Immorality Leads to Unbelief* (Chicago: Moody, 2010), 105–6.

53 See Acts 14:5–7; 16:10, 13–15, 29–33; 18:5; 28:23; 2 Cor. 10:5; Col. 4:6; Titus 1:9.

54 Mark Horne laments the fallout of Van Til's apologetic partisanship, "Not only did Van Til's method tend to make for bad communication, it also polarized the debate over apologetic methodology." "Presumptuous Presuppositions: The Apologetics of Cornelius Van Til," *Christianity Today*, February 5, 1996, 40. On the other hand, William Lane Craig makes a distinction between "*knowing* that [Christianity] is true and *showing* that it is true. We

To my knowledge, no classicist or evidentialist holds that regeneration is purely a matter of intellectual argumentation. Craig argues that the Holy Spirit's inner work and witness, rather than cold, hard rational arguments, are the prevailing catalyst and confirmation of personal conversion.[55]

Gannon Murphy models a three-fold approach. The first is to remove intellectual stumbling blocks by way of a reasoned apologetic.[56] Suppose regeneration is divorced from any leveling work in the mind and conscience. Why does the apostle Paul appeal to this sort of common ground in his sermon before the philosophers at the Areopagus (Acts 17)? Why would Paul quote Epimenides of Crete, a pagan poet, in the middle of that sermon if common ground didn't exist (v. 28)? Unless one adopts the position that Paul's apologetic was unbiblical, Acts 17 should serve as a prime example of salvaging anything of relevance to make one's case for biblical Christianity. Paul later writes, "We destroy arguments and every lofty opinion raised against the knowledge of God, and take every thought captive to obey Christ" (2 Cor. 10:5). Dismantling and destroying false arguments is part of spiritual warfare. God is sovereign. So when the Sovereign God says, "Move," we move. When he says, "Give a reasoned defense," we do just that. If God has ordained the use of means, let us use the tools that God has sanctioned to do the work he has called us to do.

Some claim that an eclectic apologetic method is absent in the teaching of Jesus. But this fundamentally misunderstands the worldview of his hearers. For example, first-century Palestinian Jews were thoroughly monotheistic. Their seventy-year Babylonian

---

know Christianity is true primarily by the self-authenticating witness of God's Spirit. We *show* Christianity is true by presenting good arguments for its central tenets." *Reasonable Faith: Christian Truth and Apologetics*, 3rd ed. (Wheaton, IL: Crossway, 2008), 58 (italics original).

55   William Lane Craig, "Classical Apologetics," in Cowan, *Five Views on Apologetics*, 28.

56   Gannon Murphy, *Voices of Reason in Christian History: Their Lives and Legacies* (Camp Hill, PA: Christian Publications, 2005), 159–60.

captivity had cured them from the outward forms of idolatry, and they had never, as a people group, flirted with atheism. So for Jesus to unleash a finely tuned teleological argument in an attempt to demonstrate the existence of God would be akin to presenting a detailed argument to die-hard Dallas Cowboys fans as to why their team deserves the title "America's Team." It would be to argue for an already assumed and accepted premise. Rather, Jesus confronted a degenerate form of monotheism, not a concoction of scientism and postmodernism. On the other hand, in twenty-first-century Western culture, an eclectic approach may be necessary for specific situations. Contemporary hearers likely need supplemental groundwork in order to seriously consider Jesus's claim to be "the truth" and the only way to God (John 14:6).

Murphy's second plank is "to ground believers in their faith so their witness may be fearless and bold (Acts 19:8; Eph. 6:19) and so they themselves are not deceived by worldly philosophies" (Col. 2:4, 8).[57] The alarming statistics on the number of students leaving the church should serve as a clarion call for increased apologetics training to ground the "why" of belief.[58] For the sake of their children, parents should take apologetics seriously. Devoting energy to preparing one's child for the labyrinth of contemporary competing viewpoints is not only noble but also necessary. John Stott puts it well, "God has revealed himself in *words* to *minds*. His revelation is a rational revelation to rational creatures."[59] As we will see, eclectic apologetics presents a powerful rebuttal against the claim that Christianity is merely an appeal to blind faith.

---

57 Murphy, *Voices of Reason in Christian History*, 161.

58 See Thom S. Rainer and Sam S. Rainer III, *Essential Church? Reclaiming a Generation of Dropouts* (Nashville: B&H, 2008). For a counterpoint suggesting that the student dropout rate is not as severe in reality as commonly suggested, see, Derik Idol, "An Assessment of Dropout Rates of Former Student Ministry Participants in Self-Identified Evangelical Churches with 500-2000 in Weekly Attendance," dissertation, Liberty University, March 2022, https://digitalcommons.liberty.edu/doctoral/3428.

59 John R. W. Stott, *Your Mind Matters: The Place of the Mind in the Christian Life* (Downers Grove, IL: IVP Books, 1972), 30.

Murphy's third and final premise for a reasoned apologetic is "to silence the attacks of the unbelieving world, which attempts to place reason and science at enmity with faith."[60] The beauty of the eclectic method is its ability to cover the breadth of the pathways of knowledge. Craig Keener lays forth another stinging indictment, "It is arrogant and unprofessional for Western scholars to reject the miraculous outright, totally ignoring the testimonies of thousands of people, based simply on their own lack of such experience."[61] From John Lennox's debunking of Stephen Jay Gould's deceptively dangerous nonoverlapping magisteria (NOMA) to William Lane Craig's use of standard big bang cosmology as a springboard for God's existence, apologists are working wonders in pushing back against secularist dogma.[62]

Here's a suggested landing point concerning the noetic effects of sin: while all persons are sinners and equally estranged from God (Rom. 3:23), not all have descended to the same levels of depravity.[63] Justin Martyr sets in perspective the *imago Dei* and the ability to reason when he writes, "In the beginning [God] made the human race with the power of thought and of choosing the truth and doing right so that all men are without excuse before God; for they have been born rational and contemplative."[64] Working

---

60 Murphy, *Voices of Reason in Christian History*, 161.

61 Keener, *Miracles*, 1:217.

62 NOMA (Nonoverlapping magisterial) refers to Stephen Jay Gould's thesis that matters of science and faith are in separate, non-overlapping categories. See John Lennox, *Seven Days That Divide the World* (Grand Rapids: Zondervan, 2011), 28; and Craig, *Reasonable Faith*, 126–56.

63 Biblical examples include God's withholding judgment against the Amorites until their iniquity is "complete" (Gen. 15:16), the depravity of Chorazin, Bethsaida, and Capernaum being worse than that of Tyre, Sidon, and Sodom (Matt. 11:21–24), and God's command to destroy specific groups (Deut. 7:1–5). For a detailed study of the command to destroy the Canaanites, see Paul Copan, *Is God a Moral Monster? Making Sense of the Old Testament God* (Grand Rapids: Baker Books, 2011), and Paul Copan and Matthew Flannagan, *Did God Really Command Genocide? Coming to Terms with the Justice of God* (Grand Rapids: Baker Books, 2014).

64 Justin Martyr, "First Apology," in Bush, *Classical Readings in Christian Apologetics*, 17.

with the knowledge that unbelief is not a purely philosophical issue allows the apologist to parry foreseeable attacks. Operating on the basis that persons are not machines and that doubts arise from other sources than just the intellect is crucial for effective apologetics. John Stott notes, "For, although men's minds are dark and their eyes are blind, although the unregenerate cannot by themselves receive or understand spiritual things 'because they are spiritually discerned' (1 Cor. 2:14), nevertheless the gospel is still addressed to their minds, since it is the divinely ordained means of opening their eyes, enlightening their minds, and saving them."[65] Information without discernment is likely to be as ineffective as it is offensive. Christians should seek the spiritual gift of discernment that will enable them to answer tough questions without pushing people away.

Emotional Fog: The Father Wound

Despite the power of human reason, the noetic effects of sin are far from minimal. Often, intellectual arguments against God's existence or the resurrection serve as smokescreens for other issues, like a guilty conscience. Douglas Groothius labels this, in a tweak of William James's famous phrase, "the will to disbelieve."[66] James Spiegel's brilliant work *The Making of an Atheist* examines the link between immorality and unbelief. Spiegel argues that, in light of the irrationality of atheism, something more than rational exploration is at play since many atheists are intellectually razor sharp, "When smart people go in irrational directions, it is time to look elsewhere than reasoning ability for an explanation."[67] Secularists attempt to make the case that atheism and agnosticism are primarily a matter of intellect and that theists (Christians specifically) have turned off the rational switch and taken a blind leap into the dark cavern of

---

65   Stott, *Your Mind Matters*, 32–33.
66   Groothius, *Christian Apologetics*, 142–46.
67   Spiegel, *Making of an Atheist*, 51.

faith. It's that subtle assumption that skepticism equals intelligence. Spiegel observes, "The human mind does not neutrally observe the world, gathering facts purely and simply without any preferences or predilections."[68] Inclination toward atheism is "a selective intellectual obtuseness or imperviousness to truths related to God, ethics, and human nature. *But the root of this obtuseness is moral in nature.*"[69] If Spiegel is even remotely correct about atheism going deeper than the intellect, what are the major contributing factors?

First, let's talk about the "father wound" that can come in the form of an absent, abusive, or aloof father figure. Alfred C. W. Davis identifies the effect of a father wound as "low self-esteem, a deep emotional pain inside and a performance orientation that makes us 'doers' rather than 'beings.'"[70] Deep down, all of us desire the approval of our father, and many of us experienced some level of a father wound. Maybe Dad rarely affirmed you or never said he was proud of you. Or Dad was around, but he was emotionally distant. Maybe he was physically abusive.

On the other hand, perhaps Dad was overbearing. I'm not talking about a dad who was merely strict, organized, or disciplined, but someone who had earned multiple PhDs in "critiqueology" and applied his expertise twenty-four hours a day, 365 days a year. No matter how much you achieved, he always had something negative to say. Rather than helpful counsel and guidance, it's a dad who wasn't able to control himself and change the channel from the station of incessant criticism. Maybe he was trying to live out his failed sports or professional aspirations through you. (Sidenote: If you're that dad, I have some helpful advice for you. Go to the closet, find your high school yearbook, locate your photo, take a moment

---

68 Spiegel, *Making of an Atheist*, 13. For a more detailed treatment of the same concept, see David A. Pailin, *The Anthropological Character of Theology: Conditioning Theological Understanding* (New York: Cambridge University Press, 1990).

69 Spiegel, *Making of an Atheist*, 56 (emphasis mine).

70 Alfred C. W. Davis, "Understanding and Healing the Father Wound," *Focus on the Family Canada*, accessed December 29, 2022.

of silence, and say goodbye to your high school self.[71] You may think you're projecting power, but you look more like Uncle Rico from *Napoleon Dynamite*, recounting his high school glory days.)

Now, a world-renowned Christian writer and apologist, Lee Strobel, was once an atheist. As Strobel sought to disprove Christianity, he discovered something about himself: his strained relationship with his own father shaped his view of God. In an interview, Strobel recounts,

> On the one hand, I had a lot of intellectual objections to Christianity. I thought that an almighty, all-powerful, all-knowing Creator of the universe was absurd. I was reinforced by the books of Bertrand Russell and Antony Flew and other famous atheists. But, there were also underlying emotional and psychological reasons as well as moral reasons. Rarely is it purely intellectual that a person becomes an atheist. Famous atheists throughout history—Camus, Sartre, Nietzsche, Freud, Voltaire, Welch, Feuerbach, O'Hair—each had a father who died when they were young, or had a terrible relationship with, or who had abandoned their family when the children were young. The implication is, "Why would you want to know a heavenly Father, if your earthly father has disappointed or hurt you?" I had a very difficult relationship with my father. *The Case for Christ* movie portrays that. That may have been something that nudged me towards atheism. There's usually a moral issue involved. Frankly, I was happy in my sin. I was a happy drunk. I was the most gregarious guy in the bar who bought pitchers of beer for everyone. It cost me a fortune. I got drunk and enjoyed it. I reveled in my sin and didn't want to come out of it.[72]

---

71   Thanks to Matt Chandler for this regular theme in his preaching to fathers.
72   Allen Satterlee, "It's Personal: Lee and Leslie Strobel on 'The Case for Christ'; The Changes in Leslie Led Lee to Investigate Christianity to Refute It," War Cry, https://magazine.thewarcry.org/stories/its-personal-lee-and-leslie-strobel-on-the-case-for-christ.

Spiegel recounts the following atheists with abusive or "weak" fathers as well:

Thomas Hobbes—was seven years old when his father deserted the family

Voltaire—had a bitter relationship with his father, whose surname (Arouet) he disowned

Baron d'Holbach—was estranged from his father and rejected his surname (Thiry)

Ludwig Feuerbach—was scandalized by his father's public rejection of his family (to live with another woman)

Samuel Butler—was physically and emotionally brutalized by his father

Sigmund Freud—had contempt for his father as a "sexual pervert" and as a weak man

H. G. Wells—despised his father who neglected the family

Madalyn Murray O'Hair—intensely hated her father, probably due to child abuse

Albert Ellis—was neglected by his father, who eventually abandoned his family[73]

Let me take a moment to pause: if this section was difficult to ingest because of your own father wound, take heart. There is hope for you. Your father wound can fester into bitterness and cynicism or become an entry point for the grace of God. Our wounds can

---

73 Spiegel, *Making of an Atheist*, 66.

harden or tenderize our hearts. I am thankful for the good news of Jesus that can transform painful scars into beautiful stories of redemption. God can give you a story for his glory.

In addition to the link between a father wound and atheism, the data suggest a possible correlation between immorality and atheism. If a person's lifestyle is driven by sexual sin, then they will be less inclined to believe in a holy God who commands a righteous lifestyle. Spiegel provides a few "CliffsNotes" on Paul Johnson's sordid *Intellectuals*:

Jean-Jacques Rousseau—intensely vain and wildly irresponsible; sired five illegitimate children and abandoned them to orphanages, which in his social context meant almost certain early death

Percy Bysshe Shelley—a chronic swindler with a ferocious temper; also an adulterer who, with three different women, fathered seven children whom he basically ignored, including one he abandoned to an orphanage, where the baby died at eighteen months

Karl Marx—egocentric, slothful, and lecherous; exploitative of friends and unfaithful to his wife; sired an illegitimate son, whom he refused to acknowledge

Henrik Ibsen—a vain, spiteful, and heartless man, caring only for money; an exploiter of women and contemptuous of the needy, even among his own family

Bertrand Russell—misogynistic and a serial adulterer; a chronic seducer of women, especially very young women, even in his old age

Jean-Paul Sartre—notorious for his sexual escapades with female students, often procured by his colleague and lover Simone de Beauvoir[74]

---

74 Spiegel, *Making of an Atheist*, 71–72. See Paul Johnson, *Intellectuals: From Marx and Tolstoy to Sartre and Chomsky* (New York: Harper & Row, 1988).

Again, unbelief is rarely *just* an intellectual issue; it is also moral and volitional. The old adage is true, "A man's morality determines his theology." If you don't believe in a holy God, you basically get a free pass when it comes to righteous living. For non-Christians to see how the logic of their own worldview suffers internal collapse—or how it is unable to support their deepest-held beliefs—is often a crucial step toward embracing Christianity. While evidence and reason play a significant role in both evangelism and discipleship, I believe that acknowledging possible nonrational causes of unbelief may be key to reaping a greater harvest.

Street Smarts: The Value of Cultural Awareness

Gordon R. Lewis recognizes that while rational arguments do not manufacture faith, they may create "the atmosphere in which belief can come to life."[75] Rational arguments serve as a tool to unlock areas of the mind that would otherwise remain closed to the claims of Christianity. Nevertheless, apologists should not only receive their "what" from Jesus but also their "how." Scandals too numerous to list sadly result in a general societal distrust of political and church leadership. To effectively communicate in this climate, apologists must realize that many of their listeners are guarded against those who expressly or tacitly say, "Trust me." So here's the uncomfortable truth: in the current cultural environment, apologists may be the most significant aspect of their apologetic. In many eyes, character and credibility precede argumentation. Trustworthiness clears the debris from the hermeneutic of distrust and opens a necessary receptivity to truth. The apologist is the showcase for that truth. Hence Scripture's emphasis on gentleness and respect (1 Peter 3:15).

Another factor is likeability. Yes, likeability. The apologist who presents an excellent case for the gospel yet lacks winsomeness (the fruit of the Holy Spirit translated through one's character) will ex-

---

75   Gordon R. Lewis, *Testing Christianity's Truth Claims: Approaches to Christian Apologetics* (Chicago: Moody, 1976), 23.

perience a lessened effectiveness. Groothius warns, "The bad man with a good argument is only half clothed. One may have a sword (arguments) but lack a shield (godly character), and thus become vulnerable and ineffective. Therefore, it is wise to consider briefly the spirituality and character of the apologist before looking at the details of apologetic method."[76] Thomas Manton, the Puritan minister, exclaimed, "Rickets cause great heads and weak feet. We are not only to dispute of the word, and talk of it, but to keep it. We must neither be all ear, nor all head, nor all tongue, but the feet must be exercised!"[77]

To be clear, there is a difference between a personal, one-on-one apologetics conversation and a public presentation. On a greater level than public, personal apologetics rises and falls with one's ability to relationally connect with others in a meaningful way. Personal skills cannot be overestimated for disarming bias against Christianity. A respectful demeanor and integrity are indispensable. Jesus speaks to the importance of a good reputation formed by good works, "You are the light of the world. A city set on a hill cannot be hidden. Nor do people light a lamp and put it under a basket, but on a stand, and it gives light to all in the house. In the same way, let your light shine before others, so that they may see your good works and give glory to your Father who is in heaven" (Matt. 5:14–16). During the 2012 presidential election, a driving factor for many American voters was whether or not the candidate "understood" them.[78] Likeability is a central ingredient in emotional perception and reception. One's character and likeability could serve as a way to prepare persons to entertain evidence for Christianity. Incorporating one's life story into one's apologetic has deep roots in Christian history and may bridge the experiential and personal

---

76   Groothuis, *Christian Apologetics*, 37.
77   Thomas Manton, *An Exposition of John 17* (Evansville, IN: Sovereign Grace Book Club, 1958), 117; quoted in Stott, *Your Mind Matters*, 82–83.
78   NPR Staff, "Presidential Politics: Does Likeability Matter?," National Public Radio, October 7, 2012, https://www.npr.org/2012/10/07/162480455/presidential-politics-does-likeability-matter.

divide. For instance, Josh McDowell once informed his audience at a major apologetics conference, "Years ago I would give the evidence and people would get saved. Now, I have to incorporate my testimony in order for people to 'connect.'"[79] Groothius says that a case for Christianity in a postmodern culture should be presented "carefully, slowly and piece by piece."[80] It does seem that conversion takes longer today than in years past.

Christians down through the ages have consistently pointed to the evidence of life change in their apologetic. Few will contest the impact of Christian martyrs on encouraging disheartened believers to remain faithful and on confirming to doubters that Christianity is worth a look. Of early Christian persecutions, Thomas Aquinas observes, "And after considering these arguments, convinced by the strength of the proof, and not by the force of arms, nor by the promise of delights, but—and this is the greatest marvel of all—amidst the tyranny of persecutions, a countless crowd of not only simple but also of the wisest men, embraced the Christian faith, which inculcates things surpassing all human understanding, curbs the pleasures of the flesh, and teaches contempt for worldly things."[81] The early church father Athanasius (c. 296–373) also appeals to the transformative power of the gospel when he says, "Or who has so

---

79   Josh McDowell, "Reaching a Postmodern Generation," *Enrichment Journal: A Journal for Pentecostal Ministry*, Summer 1999.

80   Groothius, *Christian Apologetics*, 50.

81   Thomas Aquinas, "Summa Contra Gentiles," in Bush, *Classical Readings in Christian Apologetics*, 279. Athenagoras's plea exudes this power:

> Allow me here to lift up my voice boldly in loud and audible outcry, pleading as I do before philosophic princes. For who of those that reduce syllogisms, and clear up ambiguities, and explain etymologies, or of those who teach homonyms and synonyms, and predicaments and axioms, and what is the subject and what the predicate, and who promise their disciples by these and such like instructions to make them happy: who of them have so purged their souls as, instead of hating their enemies, to love them; and, instead of speaking ill of those who have reviled them (to abstain from which of itself an evidence of no mean forbearance), to bless them; and to pray for those who plot against their lives? ("A Plea for the Christians," in Bush, *Classical Readings in Christian Apologetics*, 43–44)

rid men of the passions of the natural man, that warmongers are chaste, and murderers no longer hold the sword, and those who were formerly mastered by cowardice play the man?"[82] There seems to be a cry for authenticity in the culture, especially among younger persons.[83] Lee Strobel humorously shares why his book *The Case for Christ* became so popular. During the writing process, he feared few young people would be interested in it. Only after publication did he fully realize the combined power of a candid personal journey and substantive evidence. Yes, his book contained massive amounts of evidence from world-class scholars, but it was in the form of his personal odyssey. The combined impact of individual experience and substantive data formed a story that people could identify with.[84]

In his 1968 book, *Escape from Reason*, Francis Schaeffer recounts how many Christians he surprised by how well he connected with the culture. He even uses the phrase "far-out." You can almost feel that 1960s vibe:

> Often people say to me, "How is it that you seem to be able to communicate with these far-out people? You seem to be able to talk in such a way that they understand what you're saying, even if they do not accept it." There may be a number of reasons why this is so, but one is that I try to get them to consider the biblical system and its truth without an appeal to blind authority—that is, as though believing meant believing just because one's family did, or as though the intellect had no part in the matter.[85]

82 Athanasius, "On the Incarnation," in Bush, *Classical Readings in Christian Apologetics*, 187–88.

83 Carl F. H. Henry writes, "Contemporary philosophy's extremity is historic Christianity's opportunity." *Remaking the Modern Mind* (Grand Rapids: Eerdmans, 1946), 7.

84 Lee Strobel, "The Case for Christ" (lecture, National Apologetics Conference, Charlotte, NC, October 18–19, 2009).

85 Francis A. Schaeffer, *Escape from Reason* (Downers Grove, IL: InterVarsity, 1968), 84.

Schaeffer's story may be stating the obvious, but in order to be a persuasive apologist, one must talk about apologetics with more than just other Christian apologists. To influence non-Christians, one must actually speak with non-Christians. There always lurks the danger of becoming conversationally isolated inside a Christian bubble away from the very persons Jesus calls his followers to reach.

Murphy records the stark distinction between a culturally nimble apologist and a professional theorist, "[Van Til] conceded much in a letter he wrote to Francis Schaeffer, saying, 'You have the advantage over me. You constantly conversed with modern artists, modern existentialists, etc., as they eat at your table, study their literature. Whereas I am only a bookworm.'"[86] Let me be clear: In no way am I disparaging Van Til's character or passion for the glory of God. I only seek to illustrate the critical importance of talking with the locals and learning the culture in order to be, once again, a maximally persuasive apologist. Involvement within the culture—rather than condemning the culture from the safety of pulpits or Christian conferences—is a requirement for learning how to speak to the culture.

Given the accessibility of social media and other venues, it should be relatively easy for some Christians to locate the cultural pulse. We should strive toward James's admonition, "Know this, my beloved brothers: let every person be quick to hear, slow to speak, slow to anger" (James 1:19). Writing in 1968, Schaeffer raised the issue of Christian parents, ministers, and teachers not realizing how out of touch they were with their own students and children, not to mention those outside the church.[87] If this was the case in 1968—the year often identified as the crucial turning point of the

---

86 Murphy, *Voices of Reason in Christian History*, 3; quoting Cornelius Van Til, "Letter from Cornelius Van Til to Francis Schaeffer," *Ordained Servant* 6, no. 4 (1997): 79.

87 Murphy, *Voices of Reason in Christian History*, 94. Schaeffer identifies "speaking a foreign language" in one's attempt to communicate as hard and fast evidence of being out of touch.

cultural revolution[88]—then where is the needle today? Awareness of current scholarship is crucial to engaging with professional academics, but consistent interaction with nonacademics may be the secret sauce of truly persuasive apologetics.

Such a simple suggestion may appear less than scholarly, but the Christian apologist should seek to be characterized by the humility of Christ, who made it a point not only to associate with but also effectively communicate to societal outcasts. Christian apologists, in order to be true to their name, should follow suit. Schaeffer concludes,

> It is much more comfortable, of course, to go on speaking the gospel only in familiar phrases to the middle classes. But that would be as wrong as if, for example, Hudson Taylor had sent missionaries to China and then told them to learn only one of three separate dialects that the people spoke. In such a case, only one group out of three *could* hear the gospel. We cannot imagine Hudson Taylor being so hard-hearted. . . . In a parallel way we are being as overwhelmingly unfair, even selfish, towards our own generation, as if the missionaries had deliberately spoken in only one dialect. The reason we often cannot speak to our children, let alone other peoples, is because we have never taken time to understand how different their thought-forms are from ours.[89]

How should apologists bridge such a gap? Schaeffer suggests, "I try to approach every problem as though I were not a Christian and see what the answer would be."[90] Smart thinkers listen, and those who listen grow smarter. Listening trains us. The degree to which

---

88 See Michael T. Kaufman, *1968* (New York: Flash Point, 2009).

89 Murphy, *Voices of Reason in Christian History*, 93–94.

90 Francis A. Schaeffer, "How I Have Come to Write My Books," in *Introduction to Francis Schaeffer* (Downers Grove, IL: InterVarsity, 1974), 35; quoted in Groothius, *Christian Apologetics*, 21.

we listen—I mean, really lean into what others are saying—is one of the most accurate barometers of our love for people and our effectiveness in helping them come to know Jesus.

Remember, people are not incarnate arguments to be intellectually chided without concern for their total personhood. Loving the discipline or the fruit of the discipline more than the Author of the apologist's arguments. C. S. Lewis warns, "We may come to love knowledge—our knowing—more than the thing known: to delight not in the exercise of our talents but in the fact that they are ours, or even in the reputation they bring us. Every success in the scholar's life increases this danger."[91] If not exercised with appropriate humility, apologetics can become an idol, and the persons for whom apologetics is intended to reach can become mere props of the apologist's veiled self-promotion.

In conclusion, doubt does not necessarily equate to unbelief. Gary Habermas rightly distinguishes between *volitional unbelief* (active rejection of God's existence) and *doubt*, "Christian doubt, defined as a lack of certainty concerning the teachings of Christianity or one's relation to them, is a very common and painful problem affecting many believers. The subject is complicated by the misconceptions and caricatures concerning doubt, which tend to militate against the finding of solutions."[92] Persuasive apologetics involves directly addressing objections while remembering there may be other factors at play. Apologetic tactics should be servants rather than masters. Learn the traditional methods, and adapt them to your audience. This is the entire point of eclectic apologetics.

---

91 C. S. Lewis, *The Weight of Glory, and Other Addresses* (New York: Macmillan, 1949), 50; quoted in David K. Clark, *To Know and Love God: Method for Theology* (Wheaton, IL: Crossway Books, 2003), 211.

92 Gary R. Habermas, *Dealing with Doubt* (Chicago: Moody, 1990), 4.

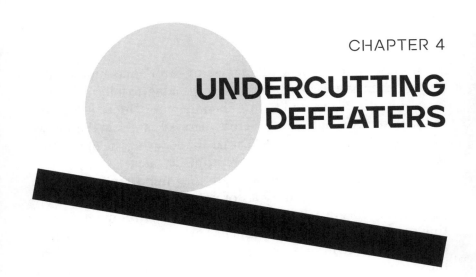

CHAPTER 4

UNDERCUTTING DEFEATERS

Have you noticed how "charged" things have become? In our increasingly fast-paced world, we are losing the ability and appetite to fully hear another person's point of view. You see it frequently on social media when people post random graphs with no documentation, external sources, and so forth or inflammatory memes that already fit their own preconceived notions. Then they sit in sniper position, ready to take out anyone who would dare question their narrative or ask, "What's your source?" If you don't fully and enthusiastically agree with their view, they'll slap a "Canceled" label on you quicker than you'll hear a "My pleasure!" at a Chick-fil-A. You know: the cable TV talking heads who continually interrupt their opponents so that fully reasoned responses, on either side of the political or religious aisle, become few and far between. Or those one-to-three-minute clips with overreaching titles like "So-and-so Destroys So-and-so" or "Person X's Response Leaves Group X Speechless." Of course, that person's point seems persuasive because the feed was cut before the other person could respond. Proverbs 18:17 is on point with this kind of stuff, "The one who states his case first seems right, until the other comes and examines him." Whether in a court of law, in friendly conversation over coffee, or in your own mind, questioning initial claims is a necessary discipline in becoming a wise person.

If there's a decreasing willingness to "hear" one another, you may not even have a chance, practically speaking, to fully make your case. How do we respond to this phenomenon? Do we just throw in the towel? Absolutely not. Here's where we can train the sinews of our minds for a sort of intellectual aikido, using the opponent's force against them through undercutting defeaters (UCD).

So what are UCDs, and why are they important? First, let's understand the two main types of defeaters and why UCDs are particularly effective in the current cultural environment. Rebutting defeaters directly attack conclusions, whereas UCDs bypass conclusions "and in some way undercut" the reasons for believing those particular conclusions.[1] In other words, UCDs undermine the entire thought process that birthed those false beliefs. Why are we focusing on UCDs? Because without them we may just end up playing a game of intellectual Whac-A-Mole. A person's worldview is what needs to be dismantled before compelling evidence for the truth of biblical Christianity finds deep receptivity. One of my friends leads a large, successful business and teaches his team, "When you choose to work on the hard stuff, you know you are dealing with the real stuff."[2] Working to undercut a false

---

1   William Lane Craig and J. P. Moreland explain, "There are at least two kinds of defeaters. First, there are rebutting defeaters, which directly attack the conclusion or thing being believed . . . a rebutting defeater would be a reason to believe *not-Q*, i.e., a reason to believe that the statue is not blue. An example would be a case where the museum director and a number of reliable, honest people assure you that the statue is grey. Second, there are undercutting defeaters. These defeaters do not directly attack the thing believed (by trying to show that it is false), but rather they attack the notion that *R* is a good reason for *Q*. *Undercutting defeaters do not attack Q directly; they attack R and in some way undercut R as a good reason for Q*. . . . In different ways, defeaters can remove the justification for a belief." William Lane Craig and J. P. Moreland, *Philosophical Foundations for a Christian Worldview*, 2nd ed. (Downers Grove, IL: IVP Academic, 2017), 145 (emphasis mine).

2   Many thanks to Bill Weisberg for this valuable leadership insight. Peggy Penjuke, "AD Members and Suppliers Celebrate Record Growth at 2018 Electrical North American Meeting," Affiliated Distributors, November 8, 2018,

narrative of the world is dealing with the real stuff. King Solomon wrote, "A wise man scales the city of the mighty and brings down the stronghold in which they trust" (Prov. 21:22). Effectiveness in agriculture depends on accurately understanding and treating the soil before reasonably expecting any level of harvest. The same is true of the human heart and mind. In the following section, we'll tease this out with a number of examples.[3]

Logical Leg Kicks

When mixed martial arts (MMA) burst onto the scene, a few techniques quickly rose to dominance. One of those was the Muay Thai leg kick. Banned in traditional karate and tae kwon do, it was absolutely devastating. Experts from other disciplines—who could echo Chris Farley's character Haru in *Beverly Hills Ninja*, "The blackness of my belt is like the inside of a coffin on a moonless night"—stood no chance against this subtle move.[4] Fighters rotate their hips, creating a whip effect in which their shins strike the opponent's leg, primarily the thigh. A properly executed leg kick sends a shockwave throughout the body. Believe me, it's not fun. After repeated blows, fighters lose mobility and become sitting ducks. Their lead leg eventually collapses, especially when they place their weight on it. When the leg collapses, so does a fighter's hope of winning. Announcers would call it "chopping down" one's opponent (although leg kicks don't have the awe factor of Chuck Norris's spinning roundhouse kick, Bruce Lee's flying side kick,

https://adhq.com/about/ad-news/ad-members-and-suppliers-celebrate-re-cord-growth-at-2018-electrical-north-american-meeting.

3   I would highly recommend Gregory Koukl's tenth-anniversary edition of *Tactics: A Game Plan for Discussing Your Christian Convictions* (Grand Rapids: Zondervan, Reflective, 2019) and Joe Carter and John Coleman's *How to Argue Like Jesus: Learning Persuasion from History's Greatest Communicator* (Wheaton, IL: Crossway, 2009). These two works heavily deal with both undercutting and rebutting defeaters.

4   *Beverly Hills Ninja*, directed by Dennis Dugan (Culver City, CA: TriStar Pictures, 1997), 88 mins.

or Mike Tyson's uppercut). Other than kickboxing, few other fighting styles were prepared to defend against this deceptively simple move.

During my first trip to the former Soviet Union, I met a Christian leader who we will call Al.[5] He had made the cut as an elite *spetsnaz* paratrooper, an enforcer for the Russian mob, and a Muay Thai fighter before becoming a Christian and then a pastor. Something tells me he has received less petty complaints from hard-to-please church members than the average American pastor does. One day, while we were moving bricks with the rest of our mission team, I reminded everyone to be careful to avoid back injury. He muttered something in return that our interpreter translated as "You cannot hurt iron."

Later that day, I questioned him about Muay Thai and the leg kick. I asked him to demonstrate his technique—a bad decision. Somehow my request for a demonstration was lost in translation, and he assumed it was a challenge to see if I could *handle* the kick. As I danced around in my fighting stance, laughing and doing my best Muhammad Ali footwork, he landed a lightning-quick leg kick on my left thigh. Immediately, a shockwave of "you may meet Jesus soon" pain shot through the right side of my body straight into what felt like my central nervous system. As my leg collapsed and I struggled to stand, he flatly responded, "This is a good kick."

Here's why it worked, and here's why I'm talking about MMA (again): if you take away your opponents' foundation, you win.[6] No matter their muscle mass or the number of "My mama eats nails" tattoos, if their foundation is dismantled, so are they. The Psalmist writes, "If the foundations are destroyed, what can the righteous

5   Because of increased governmental and cultural persecution against Christians in this part of the world, I will refrain from using his real name.

6   AintNoSunshine, "The Striking Zone: Why Leg Kicks Are Game Changers in MMA," MMA Mania, August 22, 2011, https://www.mmamania.com/2011/8/22/2373511/the-striking-zone-why-legs-kicks-are-game-changers.

do?" (Ps. 11:3). Foundation is crucial in martial arts and also in apologetics. In the following section, we'll learn how to identify a few common fallacies and, in turn, deal out logically devastating UCDs but with the tone of gentleness and respect (1 Peter 3:15).

Jesus Turning the Tables

Scenario 1: The WidowMaker

A group of Sadducees crafted a hypothetical dilemma in which a woman successively married seven brothers after each one died. Sadducees did not believe in the resurrection, which may explain why they were sad, you see. The group asked Jesus, "In the resurrection, therefore, whose wife will the woman be? For the seven had her as wife" (Luke 20:33). She sounds like the original WidowMaker. If she were alive today, no doubt the Netflix documentary about her life would appear under the More Like This tab next to *Tiger King*. Think about being the fourth, fifth, sixth, or seventh brother. Wouldn't you have thought she might be slipping something other than creamer into the coffee? I chased this rabbit down for a reason. The Sadducees were highly intelligent people. Dialogue, reason, and titanic memory powers were their everyday bread and butter. But don't miss how the absurdity of their question reveals that the question wasn't the real issue at all. Rather, the real issue was their love of money and power. Their obsession with proving Jesus wrong, fueled by their intellectual pride and moral obstinacy, are written all over this scenario.

Check out how Jesus responds, "The sons of this age marry and are given in marriage, but those who are considered worthy to attain to that age and to the resurrection from the dead neither marry nor are given in marriage" (vv. 34–35). Instead of giving a straightforward answer, Jesus corrects their presuppositions concerning the resurrection. First, the question of whose wife the woman will be erroneously assumes marriage and weddings will take place in heaven. It's a false premise. Heaven isn't a sanctified version of *The Bachelor* or *The Bachelorette*. So there's no need for the widow to worry about who she'll call "sweetheart" for eternity.[7] Jesus corrects the question before answering it. You can almost imagine Buddy the Elf in the bleachers howling at the Sadducees, "You sit on a throne of lies!"[8]

Second, Jesus goes beyond the snare of their specific question to undercut their entire worldview, "For [those who attain the resurrection from the dead] cannot die anymore, because they are equal to angels and are sons of God, being sons of the resurrection. But that the dead are raised, even Moses showed, in the passage about the bush, where he calls the Lord the God of Abraham and the God of Isaac and the God of Jacob. Now he is not God of the dead, but of the living, for all live to him" (vv. 36–38). See what just happened? Jesus fundamentally undercuts the Sadducees' entire theological system by appealing to the Hebrew Bible. On the one hand, the Sadducees didn't even believe in the resurrection. On the other hand, Jesus sees their ambush and turns the tables on them by appealing to a proper interpretation of Moses's writings in the Old Testament. The scribes then verbalize what everyone present was already thinking, "Then some of the scribes answered, 'Teacher, you have spoken well.' For they no longer dared to ask him any question" (v. 39).

Why did Jesus take this route? Gullibly answering a question with a false premise is supporting foolishness. Jesus previously warned the disciples against unwisely sparring with those who exhibit no desire for truth (Matt. 7:6).[9] Here, Jesus turns the hollow

---

7   Thaddeus J. Williams, "What You Can Learn from the Logic of Jesus," Crosswalk.com, February 24, 2017, https://www.crosswalk.com/faith/bible-study/what-you-can-learn-from-the-logic-of-jesus.html.

8   See *Elf*, directed by Jon Favreau (Burbank, CA: New Line Cinema, 2003), 97 mins.

9   R. T. France comments, "Holy and valuable things should be given only to those able to appreciate them. No specific application is indicated, but we may remember that there is a time to speak and a time to be silent (Ec. 3:7). God's truth must not be exposed unnecessarily to abuse and mockery." "Matthew," in *New Bible Commentary*, ed. D. A. Carson, R. T. France, J. A. Motyer, and G. J. Wenham, 4th ed. (Downers Grove, IL: InterVarsity, 1994), 913.

"Whose wife will she be?" inquiry around on the questioners. Jesus never let those who use sacred truths as rhetorical bludgeons to get away with it unscathed.[10]

Scenario 2: A House Divided
Mark 3 captures Jesus's rising fame. With popularity comes increased criticism:

> And the scribes who came down from Jerusalem were saying, "He is possessed by Beelzebul," and "by the prince of demons he casts out the demons." And he called them to him and said to them in parables, "How can Satan cast out Satan? If a kingdom is divided against itself, that kingdom cannot stand. And if a house is divided against itself, that house will not be able to stand. And if Satan has risen up against himself and is divided, he cannot stand, but is coming to an end. But no one can enter a strong man's house and plunder his goods, unless he first binds the strong man. Then indeed he may plunder his house." (vv. 22–27)

Notice how Jesus identifies the scribes' error. He does not defend his messiahship. Neither does he exhibit an emotional knee-jerk reaction to their insults. He merely undercuts their specific accusation. "If you claim I'm a demon wrangler because I'm in cahoots with Satan, then it would make sense to sling little devils into people rather than cast them out of people." No coherent person destabilizes his or her own organization. Likewise, there is a necessity for unity even in Satan's kingdom, "And if Satan has risen up against himself and is divided, he cannot stand, but is coming to an end" (v. 26). The scribes allow their jealousy to cloud their intellect. Jesus lovingly levels their question with a laser-guided UCD.

---

10   See Matt. 22:34–45; Mark 10:2–12; 11:27–33; Luke 11:37–12:34; 20:1–44; John 18:19–24.

Scenario 3: The King and Bling, of Coins and Caesar
In this account, Jesus skillfully navigates the radioactive topic of taxes with a brilliant UCD that flips the script and leaves the hearers marveling.

> Then the Pharisees went and plotted how to entangle him in his words. And they sent their disciples to him, along with the Herodians, saying, "Teacher, we know that you are true and teach the way of God truthfully, and you do not care about anyone's opinion, for you are not swayed by appearances. Tell us, then, what you think. Is it lawful to pay taxes to Caesar, or not?" But Jesus, aware of their malice, said, "Why put me to the test, you hypocrites? Show me the coin for the tax." And they brought him a denarius. And Jesus said to them, "Whose likeness and inscription is this?" They said, "Caesar's." Then he said to them, "Therefore render to Caesar the things that are Caesar's, and to God the things that are God's." When they heard it, they marveled. And they left him and went away. (Matt. 22:15–22)

In what may be one of Jesus's most famous dialogues, pay close attention to his opponents' real motive, "Then the Pharisees went and plotted how to entangle him in his words" (v. 15). Unfortunately, this was a theme with both the Pharisees and the scribes, "As he went away from there, the scribes and the Pharisees began to press him hard and to provoke him to speak about many things, lying in wait for him, to catch him in something he might say" (Luke 11:53–54). Let's be clear: these were not honest quests for truth. Part of being wise as a serpent is recognizing that not all who ask are really searching for truth. Delusion is nowhere better illustrated than the creation believing it has a chance to snare the Creator. Nevertheless, human nature tends to overexaggerate its own intellectual sophistication while simultaneously underestimating its own depravity.

So back to the story. Should we pay taxes to Caesar or refuse to file? It seems like these are the two and only horns of the dilemma. Jesus could have launched into a lengthy monologue on natural law, taxation policies, tyrannical empires, and so on. But he takes a different direction. Why did Jesus ask for a coin? Because Caesar's image was on the coin. Then Jesus makes his move. If Caesar's image is on the coin, render unto Caesar what is Caesar's. But more significant than that, whose image is in and on you? Every Jew present would have immediately made the connection to Genesis 1, where humans are created in the image of God, "So God created man in his own image, in the image of God he created him; male and female he created them" (Gen. 1:27). If you're made in God's image, then what should be rendered to him? You! Since God has created you in his image, you are his. This reality speaks to both value and responsibility—value because God doesn't make any junk, and responsibility because image-bearers represent the Creator. Let Caesar have his cold little coin, but let God have your heart.

Jesus's answer to the Pharisees had to sting, especially because he had just publicly exposed their moral corruption (Matt. 22:18). "You're trying to nail me with a false dilemma, which I just split and undercut. But there's a far bigger issue at play here than your rhetorical gymnastics. Your malice has marred your soul, and you must realize your guilt before the One who knows all things." You get the gist. Jesus's answer is so profound that "when they heard it, they marveled. And they left him and went away" (v. 22). Not only were their intellectual satellites knocked offline, but their desperate need for a spiritual heart transplant could no longer be denied.

Throughout Jesus's ministry, the Pharisees showed a pattern of hardened resistance to heart-revealing truth. Most of the Pharisees relished cognitively accessing biblical content, but they were never really interested in the truth getting into them. They were merely trying to leverage theological angles to discredit Jesus, thereby justifying their own hypocrisy in the eyes of the people.[11] Jesus's repeated woes against the Pharisees were due in part to their chronic pattern of shrouding corrupt intentions with deceptively formulated theological queries (Luke 11:39, 42–43). By no means is this to say that all questions represent a calcified heart of unbelief. But suppose the Pharisaic red herrings and smokescreens are a cautionary tale. In that case, any version of intellectual pretext designed to shield oneself from moral accountability invites the same pronouncement from Jesus.

Undercutting Defeaters in Rational Dialogue and the Pursuit of Happiness

Scenario 1: Plato and the Law of Noncontradiction
We've probably all heard it before, "There is no absolute truth! There's your truth, and then there's my truth." In response, we can tap into the brilliance of Plato's dialogues. Protagoras is trying to convince Socrates that each person's opinion is equally true:

Socrates: So you believe that each man's opinion is as good as anyone else's?

Protagoras: That's correct.

Socrates: How do you make a living?

Protagoras: I am a teacher.

Socrates: I find this very puzzling. You admit you earn money teaching, but I cannot imagine what you could possibly teach anyone. After all, you admit that each person's opinion is as good as anyone else's. This means that what your students believe is as good as anything

---

11   See Matt. 9:11; 12:14, 24, 38; 16:1; 19:3; 22:34–36, 41–46; Mark 12:13; Luke 6:7; 11:53; 16:14; John 11:47–57.

you could possibly teach them. Once they learn that each person is the measure of all things, what possible reason would they have to pay you for any further lessons? How can you possibly teach them anything once they learn that their opinions are as true as yours?[12]

See what Socrates does here? He applies an embarrassingly effective UCD to Protagoras's claim that any opinion is as good as any other. "If that's true, Protagoras, then why are you trying to convince me of the superiority of your opinion that all opinions are just as good as the other?" It's sort of like Obi-Wan Kenobi's smart-sounding quip, "Only a Sith deals in absolutes."[13] But wait. Isn't that an absolute statement? It seems Obi-Wan's logical skills aren't quite as sharp as his lightsaber. I'm thankful for Greg Koukl's illustration on this point regarding morality:

> As I have written elsewhere, "A person can wax eloquent with you in a discussion on moral relativism, but he will complain when somebody cuts in front of him in line. He'll object to the unfair treatment he gets at work and denounce injustice in the legal system. He'll criticize crooked politicians who betray the public trust and condemn intolerant fundamentalists who force their moral views on others."

---

12 Ronald H. Nash, *Life's Ultimate Questions: An Introduction to Philosophy* (Grand Rapids: Zondervan, 1999), 230. We also see this in Plato's *Sophist*, with a fascinating conversation between the Stranger and Theaetetus. The Stranger is a Clint Eastwood drifter type who, no matter where he travels, becomes embroiled in deep discussions (rather than gunfights) with those he meets, "*Str[anger]*. And surely contend we must in every possible way against him who would annihilate knowledge and reason and mind, and yet ventures to speak confidently about anything. *Theaet[etus]*. Yes, with all our might." *The Dialogues of Plato*, trans. Benjamin Jowett (New York: Horace Liverwright, 1954), 488.

13 *Star Wars, Episode III: Revenge of the Sith*, directed by George Lucas (San Francisco: Lucasfilm Ltd., 2005), 140 mins.

I think this was Paul's point in Romans 2:1 when he wrote, "Therefore you are without excuse, every [one] of you who passes judgment, for in that you judge another, you condemn yourself; for you who judge practice the same things." Paul argued that those who set up their own morality are still faulted by their own code. Their "excuse" commits suicide.[14]

These are textbook examples of sawing off the branch you are sitting on.[15] Contrary to Protagoras's self-defeating statement, truth is what corresponds to reality.

Scenario 2: Ayn Rand, Happiness, and Parental Duty

If you're not familiar with the works of Ayn Rand, do yourself a favor and check out the book or movie *Atlas Shrugged*. Regardless of the degree to which you agree or disagree with Rand's political philosophy, her ability to paint a possible future world with veins of the past is simply brilliant. She does a marvelous job of flaying open the dangers of Marxist collectivism. Her mantra in her book *Anthem*—"We are one in all and all in one. There are no men but only the great we, one, indivisible and forever"—highlights the danger of eradicating the value of the individual.[16] However, her notorious struggle to make a case for parental duty is well documented:

> Happiness is the successful state of life; pain is an agent of death. Happiness is that state of consciousness which proceeds from the achievement of one's values. A morality that dares to tell you to find happiness in the renunciation of your happiness—to value the failure of your values—is an insolent negation of morality. A

---

14 Koukl, *Tactics*, 125; quoting Francis J. Beckwith and Gregory Koukl, *Relativism: Feet Firmly Planted in Mid-Air* (Grand Rapids: Baker Books, 1998), 143.
15 C. S. Lewis, *Mere Christianity*, HarperCollins ed. (New York: HarperOne, 2000), 48.
16 Ayn Rand, *Anthem* (1938; reprint, New York: Millennium, 2014), 4.

doctrine that gives you, as an ideal, the role of a sacrificial animal seeking slaughter on the altars of others, is giving you *death* as your standard. . . . The purpose of morality is to teach you, not to suffer and die, but to enjoy yourself and live.[17]

Several years later, Rand crystallized this sentiment into possibly her most famous claim, "Accept the fact that the achievement of your happiness is the only *moral* purpose of your life, and that *happiness*—not pain or mindless self-indulgence—is the proof of your moral integrity, since it is the proof and the result of your loyalty to the achievement of your values."[18] Rand's firsthand experience of Communist coercion in the Soviet Union was likely a major contributing factor to her ethical value structure.

At first glance, Rand's claims sound like rocket fuel for liberty lovers. However, when examined a bit closer, we see several noticeable gaps. First, championing personal happiness as the moral purpose of one's life may sound noble but is fundamentally arbitrary. Her statement ruggedly asserts moral demands without a reasoned foundation for morality. How so? As an atheist, Rand would be forced to answer Arthur Allen Leff's "Sez who?" with "Me" in reference to ultimate moral authority.[19] Who is Rand—or anyone, for that matter—to pontificate so authoritatively on matters of purpose? Whether of an Epicurean, Randesque, or neurotic flavor, happiness boils down to subjective, whimsical fluctuations.

---

17 Ayn Rand, *Atlas Shrugged* (New York: Random House, 1957), 940–41.

18 Ayn Rand, *For the New Intellectual: The Philosophy of Ayn Rand* (New York: Random House, 1961), 179. Her character John Galt continues, "But neither life nor happiness can be achieved by the pursuit of irrational whims. Just as man is free to attempt to survive in any random manner, but will perish unless he lives as his nature requires, so he is free to seek his happiness in any mindless fraud, but the torture of frustration is all he will find, unless he seeks the happiness proper to man" (123).

19 Arthur Allen Leff, "Unspeakable Ethics, Unnatural Law," *Duke Law Journal* 6 (1979): 1229; quoted in David Baggett and Jerry L. Walls, *Good God: The Theistic Foundations of Morality* (Oxford: Oxford University Press, 2011), 3.

Rand's moralistic dogmatism is paralyzed unless one is willing to
adopt the Nietzschean ethics[20] expressed in Eric Hoffer's striking
statement that the "quality of ideas seems to play a minor role in
mass movement leadership. What counts is the arrogant gesture,
the complete disregard of the opinion of others, the single-handed
defiance of the world."[21] Ironically, it was precisely this sort of
domineering totalitarianism exemplified by the Soviet Union that
Rand reacted so strongly against.

Second, when applied to parental duty, Rand's position carries
troubling implications for children. We may pose the following
challenges: Since child-raising is physically, emotionally, mentally,
and financially challenging, then wouldn't abandoning one's child
be ethically permissible? Being awakened at 3:00 a.m. by infantile
shrieks, finding Cheerios in seemingly inaccessible places, or
changing Chernobylesque diapers are unlikely roadmaps to happiness for most persons. One could counter with an argument for
delayed gratification, but that falters if the child grows up to lead a
life of crime and brings family shame, financial disaster, and even
physical harm or death to the parent. Arguing for parental duty
based on the delayed gratification of the child's future success is
more of a shot in the dark than an actual argument.

Rand's comment that "a morality that dares to tell you to find
happiness in the renunciation of your happiness" is likely aimed
at Christianity.[22] She adamantly stresses the moral necessity of

---

20 Nietzsche says, "To prepare a *reversal of values* for a certain strong kind of
    man of the highest spirituality and strength of will and to this end slowly
    and cautiously to unfetter a host of instincts now kept in check. . . . I write
    for a species of man that does not yet exist: for the 'masters of the earth.'
    Religions, as consolations and relaxations, dangerous: man believes he has a
    right to take his ease. In Plato's *Theages* it is written: 'Each one of us would
    like to be master over all men, if possible, and best of all God.' This atti-
    tude must exist again." Friedrich Nietzsche, *The Will to Power*, trans. Walter
    Kaufmann and R. J. Hollingdale, ed. Walter Kaufman (New York: Random
    House, 1967), 503.
21 Eric Hoffer, *The Passionate State of Mind* (Titusville, NJ: Hopewell, 2006), 181.
22 Rand, *Atlas Shrugged*, 940.

rejecting any ethical structure that impinges on one's happiness. But she omits establishing the grounds of her claim. Without an objective standard, Rand is simply pontificating and asserting her own authority. Ironically, she commits a fallacy similar to the ones committed by her former Soviet overlords.

Undercutting Defeaters in Arguments Against Faith

Scenario 1: "Faith Is Irrational; Believing in God Is Checking Your Brain at the Door."

The objection that faith is irrational takes many forms, but the basic premise is that belief in God is irresponsible, irrational, ignorant, etc. Simply put, Christians are thinking wrongly. How do you respond? One way is by asking something like this, "If God does not exist, on what basis can you rely on reason?" Think about it: atheistic naturalism holds that everything, including your mind, developed by chance. How can a thing formed through randomness be a reliable logical processor? If God does not exist, then we make an unwarranted assumption that we can really know anything at all. Richard Purtill writes, "So a mindless nature could produce mind only by chance. But if mind is only a chance product of nature, how can we trust our reasoning powers, how can we expect our minds to give us the truth about anything?"[23] C. S. Lewis puts it this way, "No thought is valid if it can be fully explained as the result of irrational causes."[24]

See what's going on here? The atheist is seeking to rebut belief in God by appealing to reason. This is precisely where we apply a UCD. We question reason itself on an atheistic worldview. In the words of A. J. Hoover, atheistic naturalism is a "smuggler's civilization, since it continues to nourish itself on values derived

---

23 Richard L. Purtill, *C. S. Lewis's Case for the Christian Faith* (San Francisco: Harper & Row, 1981), 23; quoted in Gary R. Habermas, *The Risen Jesus and Future Hope* (New York: Rowman & Littlefield, 2003), 55.

24 C. S. Lewis, *Miracles* (New York: Macmillan, 1960), 14–15, 26; quoted in Habermas, *Risen Jesus and Future Hope*, 54.

from another worldview. . . . Naturalism also smuggles in values and can't subsist without them."[25] While Hoover is specifically referring to moral values, his point can also be applied to reason, which is the mechanism through which we arrive at all sorts of judgments. Richard Taylor frames the point brilliantly:

> Thus the naturalists seem to be caught in a trap. If they are consistent with their naturalistic presuppositions, they must assume that our human cognitive faculties are a product of chance, purposeless forces. But if this is so, they appear grossly inconsistent when they place so much trust in those faculties. But . . . if they assume that their cognitive faculties are trustworthy and do provide accurate information about the world, they seem compelled to abandon one of the cardinal presuppositions of metaphysical naturalism and to conclude that their cognitive faculties were formed as a result of the activity of some purposeful, intelligent agent.[26]

Bottom line: if God does not exist, we have little *reason* to trust our ability to reason. Even if atheism is in fact true, *there's no reason to think that it's true*. Atheists cannot consistently assume the intellectual high ground and demand reasons and proofs from theists because a naturalistic account of reason is about as reliable as a Ford Pinto gas tank. We are free to believe reason got here by chance (nonrational causes), but then there is no basis to believe that very statement.[27]

---

25 A. J. Hoover, *The Case for Christian Theism: An Introduction to Apologetics* (Grand Rapids: Baker, 1976), 105.

26 Richard Taylor, *Metaphysics*, 2nd ed. (Englewood Cliffs, NJ: Prentice Hall, 1974), 59. Many thanks to Dr. Matthew J. Coombe for elaborating on this point; "Presupposition and Apologetic Method," lecture, Liberty Baptist Theological Seminary, Lynchburg, VA, April 11, 2012.

27 Coombe, "Presupposition and Apologetic Method."

Scenario 2: "Hypocrites in the Church Disprove Christianity."
The charge that hypocrites in the church disprove Christianity is a common objection, especially when one is actively inviting people to church services. Before we dive into the particulars of a response, remember that if gentleness and respect were ever needed, they're desperately needed here. We are all probably aware of people who use the "hypocrites in the church" objection to shield themselves or self-soothe from painful memories. Some carry wounds from church splits, pastoral moral failure, or downright mean-hearted church members. Talk to any pastor's kid, and they'll likely admit to having seen at least some of the latter, even if they've processed those experiences and emotions in a healthy way. If you sense any level of teeth-gnashing vitriol against the church, there may be more than meets the eye. If that is what is really brewing below the surface, then you're in no way dealing *exclusively* with an intellectual objection to the claims of Christianity. You're speaking with a deeply wounded person. Remember, there's almost always *more* to the question than the question itself.

As Christians, we believe in living consistent lives. God's unchanging nature and attributes form the template for the Christian life. Since God is holy, we should walk in holiness. The apostle Paul urges the Philippian believers, "Only let your manner of life be worthy of the gospel of Christ" (Phil. 1:27). Jesus's disciple John uses the same theme, "Little children, let us not love in word or talk but in deed and in truth" (1 John 3:18). Even though we all appreciate and strive for consistency in our lives, none of us always reach it.

Here's a possible response to someone who says that hypocrisy in the church is a reason not to believe. First, agree with them about hypocrites in the church. No, this is not a typo. You read it correctly. Why should you agree with them that (some) professing Christians are hypocrites? Because it's true! There *are* hypocrites in the church. Remember, apologetics is giving a reasoned defense for the hope that lies within us. Our hope is in Jesus Christ and him alone, not in the behavior of professing Christians. Second, say something like this, "Not only do I agree with you that there are some hypocrites in the church, but you actually agree with Jesus because he *said* there would be hypocrites in the church!" Jesus says, "Not everyone who says to me, 'Lord, Lord,' will enter the kingdom of heaven, but the one who does the will of my Father who is in heaven. On that day many will say to me, 'Lord, Lord, did we not prophesy in your name, and cast out demons in your name, and do many mighty works in your name?' And then will I declare to them, 'I never knew you; depart from me, you workers of lawlessness'" (Matt. 7:21–23). You see, Jesus not only recognized the hypocrites of his day but foretold that they would be fruitful and multiply. They would last until the day when every hidden thing would be brought into the light. Here's the point: if Jesus said there would be hypocrites (and there are hypocrites), then hypocrites *confirm* rather than *deny* Jesus's teachings.

Third, according to Jesus, people won't get away with their hypocrisy. Rather than running roughshod over others and ultimately profiting from a double-faced life, hypocrites will face, in the words of R. G. Lee's famous sermon, "payday someday."[28] If you see hypocrites in the church as a matter of injustice, be assured that Jesus promises to make everything right in the end. He will deliver justice with pinpoint accuracy.

Fourth and finally, why let a hypocrite determine the direction of your life? Why allow him or her to affect your eternity? What about hypocrites in the church? The late D. James Kennedy once said, "Well, there's always room for one more."[29] At a certain point, we all have to admit that none of us are *entirely* consistent. It's one thing to recognize the behaviors in others that we disagree with. It's an entirely new level of maturity when we notice and admit our

28   See Luke Holmes, "Famous Baptist Sermons: Payday Someday by RG Lee," *SBC Voices* (blog), November 30, 2020, https://sbcvoices.com/famous-bap-tist-sermons-payday-someday-by-rg-lee.
29   R. C. Sproul, "Is the Church Full of Hypocrites?," Ligonier, October 29, 2009, https://www.ligonier.org/learn/articles/church-full-hypocrites. Sproul goes on to note, "[Kennedy] cautioned people that if they found a perfect church, they ought not to join it, since that would ruin it."

own inconsistencies. Few things are more burdensome than our conscience repeatedly whispering, "Hypocrite!" It's not a problem that we're bothered by our inconsistency. It indicates properly functioning cognitive and moral faculties. The danger is not ultimately when we're inconsistent but when our conscience is not pricked when we behave at odds with what we claim to believe. We've likely seen or experienced the internal misery this creates. When the rooster crowed its warning signal of hypocrisy, the apostle Peter "went out and wept bitterly" (Matt. 26:75; Luke 22:62). On the other hand, traitors, turncoats, and hypocrites are pitied almost as much as they are universally despised. Being disturbed by our depravity can actually be the first step toward repentance and restoration.

It's one thing to say, "I don't agree with what he or she is doing." It's another to say, "But then again, I don't even agree with everything that I do." If we only stay in the first category and never crack the door to the second, we're likely self-absorbed rather than self-aware. Here's where both the hypocrite and the hypocrite police can gain rich insight from the apostle Paul's transparency, "For I do not do the good I want, but the evil I do not want is what I keep on doing. . . . Wretched man that I am! Who will deliver me from this body of death? Thanks be to God through Jesus Christ our Lord! So then, I myself serve the law of God with my mind, but with my flesh I serve the law of sin" (Rom. 7:19, 24–25).

It's not hypocrisy to *struggle* against sin. It's actually a sign of spiritual life. If there is no struggle, there may be no spiritual life. Hypocrisy is saying that we have no sin. The Christian life is one of struggle against the world, the flesh, and the devil (Eph. 2:1–3; 1 John 2:15–17). Jonathan Edwards paints the difference between hypocrites and genuine Christians in these terms, "The former rejoices in himself; self is the first foundation of his joy: the latter rejoices in God."[30] If you're bothered by hypocrites, so is Jesus. Don't worry, he'll deal with them. But what about you? It's far more

---

30 Jonathan Edwards, *The Works of Jonathan Edwards*, vol. 2, *Religious Affections*, ed. John E. Smith (Peabody, MA: Hendrickson, 2005), 249.

challenging to admit the plank in our own eye than to call out the speck of sawdust in another's eye (Matt. 7:3–5).

Undercutting Defeaters and World Religions

Scenario 1: Islam, Compassion, and the Crucifixion of Jesus
One of the central divergences between Islam and biblical Christianity revolves around the crucifixion of Jesus. Contrary to the accounts of the gospel writers, as well as first-century Jewish and Gentile opponents of Christianity, the majority Islamic position is that the Qur'an claims Jesus was never crucified:

> And [for] their saying, "Indeed, we have killed the Messiah, Jesus, the son of Mary, the messenger of Allah." And they did not kill him, nor did they crucify him; but [another] was made to resemble him to them. And indeed, those who differ over it are in doubt about it. They have no knowledge of it except the following of assumption. And they did not kill him, for certain. Rather, Allah raised him to Himself. And ever is Allah Exalted in Might and Wise. And there is none from the People of the Scripture but that he will surely believe in Jesus before his death. And on the Day of Resurrection he will be against them a witness. (4:157–59)[31]

The Qur'an indicates rather clearly that God did not allow Jesus to suffer at the hands of his enemies. Someone *was* crucified, but it wasn't Jesus. Moreover, the majority Islamic interpretation is that Jesus ascended to heaven without being killed by his enemies.[32]

---

31 For ease of access, I am using the widely available Sahih International version. https://quran.com.

32 Although this is the majority view, some contend the Qur'an teaches that Jesus did in fact die. Gabriel Said Reynolds, "The Muslim Jesus: Dead or Alive?," *Bulletin of the School of Oriental and African Studies* 72, no. 2 (2009): 237–58.

Here's where you can apply a respectful UCD: Why would Jesus's death be irreconcilable with the power of God? What if a shameful death was part one of the story? What if suffering precedes a greater glory? As you may know, every surah, or chapter, begins with the phrase "In the name of Allah, the compassionate (entirely merciful), the merciful (especially merciful)." If one of Allah's qualities is compassion and mercy, then what greater compassion and mercy than a voluntary, substitutionary sacrifice for the sins of humanity? Issa, or Jesus, himself says in John 15:12–13, "This is my commandment, that you love one another as I have loved you. Greater love has no one than this, that someone lay down his life for his friends." I realize that most Muslims believe the apostle Paul was a corrupter of Jesus's teaching,[33] but it does seem that he furthers Jesus's idea of love and sacrifice, "For while we were still weak, at the right time Christ died for the ungodly. For one will scarcely die for a righteous person—though perhaps for a good person one would dare even to die—but God shows his love for us in that while we were still sinners, Christ died for us. Since, therefore, we have now been justified by his blood, much more shall we be saved by him from the wrath of God" (Rom. 5:6–9). Paul's point is that Jesus did not love us because we were righteous. Quite the contrary! He *died* for us even when we were unrighteous.

Amar Djaballah argues, "The Christian understanding of the cross must also be clarified. Jesus' death is not evidence of God's failure, but instead, it is the very wisdom and power of God rooted in the plan of God before the foundations of the world to save his people from their sins (cf. Acts 2:22–23; 4:27–28; Mt 1:21). The Muslim rejection of the reality of the cross is often backed by objections such as, 'How could God allow his faithful prophet (let alone his Son!) to be killed in so unjust and degrading a manner? Why

---

33   David Wood, "David Wood vs. Shabir Ally: 'Does Paul Give Us the Truth about Jesus?,'" *Answering Muslims: The Islamoblog of Acts 17 Apologetics*, October 4, 2015, http://www.answeringmuslims.com/2015/10/david-wood-vs-shabir-ally-does-paul.html.

was he not rescued?'"[34] Go with me here for a moment. If there's a chance that Christians are even remotely correct about Issa, then his voluntary sacrificial death could be the very thing that defines and illustrates compassion and mercy. Biblical Christians and committed Muslims both agree that God is a righteous judge who must punish sin. They also both agree that God is compassionate and merciful. In the crucifixion of Jesus, we see the ultimate display of love and compassion. In the resurrection, we see the ultimate power of God. As to the voluntary nature of Jesus's death, the Lord says, "No one takes it from me, but I lay it down of my own accord. I have authority to lay it down, and I have authority to take it up again. This charge I have received from my Father" (John 10:18). It's one thing to *say* God is compassionate, merciful, and all powerful. It's a different matter altogether to have an example from God that demonstrates those values in a profoundly deep and meaningful way. Even more so if the Suffering Servant is God in the flesh (Isa. 53; John 1:1–5).

If Jesus is not the sacrificial lamb who satisfies the moral demands of God's law, then the burden rests on our own shoulders. Committed Muslims are very much aware of this. As Suzanne Haneef notes, "No Muslim, even the best among them, imagines that he is guaranteed Paradise; on the contrary the more conscientious and God-fearing one is, the more he is aware of his own shortcomings and weaknesses. Therefore the Muslim, knowing that God alone controls life and death, and that death may come to him at any time, tries to send on ahead for his future existence such deeds as will merit the pleasure of his Lord, so that he can look forward to it with hope for His mercy and grace."[35] For Muslims, the

---

34   Amar Djaballah, "Jesus in Islam," *Southern Baptist Journal of Theology* 8, no. 1 (2004): 25, https://sbts-wordpress-uploads.s3.amazonaws.com/equip/uploads/2010/02/sbjt_081_djaballah.pdf.

35   Suzanne Haneef, *What Everyone Should Know about Islam and Muslims* (Chicago: Kazi, 1979), 37; quoted in James W. Sire, *The Universe Next Door: A Basic Worldview Catalog*, 5th ed. (Downers Grove, IL: IVP Academic, 1009), 261.

outcome on judgment day depends on whether one's good deeds surpass one's bad deeds. Surah 23:102–3 reads, "And those whose scales are heavy [with good deeds]—it is they who are the successful. But those whose scales are light—those are the ones who have lost their souls, [being] in Hell, abiding eternally."[36] Salvation, then, is a tedious affair with eternal ramifications. But the haunting question is whether we're even able to balance the scales.

Indeed, are we able to balance the scales? Bible-believing Christians believe that salvation is by grace alone, through faith alone, in Jesus alone (Eph. 2:8–9). This is the fundamental difference between Christianity and Islam (and all other world religions, for that matter). It is here that you can walk through the life of Jesus and show how his works and words fulfill all moral or religious requirements. Jesus's scale is maxed out by the weightiness of his righteousness. To consistently cling to both God's compassion and righteousness, one a needs a lynchpin that can reconcile both. Jesus fits the bill.

Scenario 2: Hinduism, Rebirth, and Morality

In Hinduism (and in Eastern thought in general), pain and suffering are assumed to be staple ingredients in the fabric of the universe. The word *samsara* is descriptive of the continuous cycle of life, death, and reincarnation or rebirth. Imagine a "wheel of suffering" wherein millions of rebirths occur, all exclusively depending on people's performance in past lives. Karma is essentially the moral law of cause and effect of caste-based duty.[37] It exacts a one-to-one reciprocation of one's deeds, whether they be "good" or "bad." Karma and one's caste are inseparable. Salvation in this system is "emancipation (*moksha*) from this morass, an escape from the impermanence that is an inherent feature of mundane existence."[38] How does a person escape this endless wheel of suffering? By working off past misdeeds.

---

36 The same sentiment is reflected in Surah 7:7–8.

37 Winfried Corduan, *Neighboring Faiths: A Christian Introduction to World Religions*, 2nd ed. (Downers Grove, IL: IVP Academic, 2012), 278.

38 Arthur Llewellyn Basham, "Hinduism," Britannica, last modified August 14, 2019, https://www.britannica.com/topic/Hinduism.

How? There's only one way: you suffer. That's it. No grace or mercy, only the crushing wheels of inexorable and mechanistic suffering. Your own suffering is the only accepted currency.

In the West, the term *karma* often carries a rather lighthearted meaning. It's the prospect of getting another chance after death or the smug feeling of satisfaction one gets from watching a YouTube video of a road-raged driver immobilizing his own vehicle while illegally jumping a curb in rush-hour traffic. However, in Eastern thought, karma is cosmic slavery.[39]

Here's where we can suggest several UCD probes. First, if our *present* situations are solely a result of our performance in past lives, why should we feel compassion for others? Second, if people are suffering from abuse, physical handicap, or painful disease, is it not *because* they are being repaid for what *they have done*? Wouldn't their present suffering simply be justice served cold? Third, if I were to intervene to relieve their suffering, I would, in effect, be hurting rather than helping. If the debt of bad karma can only be "worked off" by suffering, then rescuing a person out of their suffering isn't helping them at all. Instead, it's delaying the inevitable if they ever hope to escape the wheel of suffering.

In my estimation, this view is morally problematic. For example, consider children who are suffering. Since I am a Christian, I am going to presuppose that helping orphans in their time of need is morally praiseworthy.[40] Moreover, to ignore destitute orphans when in a position to help is morally abhorrent. Average secularized Westerners, who unknowingly carry bits and pieces of a Christian memory, will usually respond positively to work like this. They assume most everyone views assisting orphans as a good thing. They reach these conclusions a priori for primarily two reasons:

---

39 Corduan, *Neighboring Faiths*, 279.
40 If pressed, I'll respond precisely with that basic presupposition. If someone challenges the presupposition, we could be dealing with a textbook social Darwinist. If so, don't be surprised if you hear offhand Malthusian-infused comments about "useless eaters" and other dismissive ideas against all persons having intrinsic value.

(1) because a Judeo-Christian worldview shaped Western culture with its categories for the proper care of children; and (2) because their God-given conscience is still functional (at least concerning children who have already been born). However, not all worldviews have the same perspective. It is here that we have an opportunity to lovingly suggest a UCD to our Hindu friends.

Again, samsara is morally problematic, especially with respect to children. If alleviating another's suffering is counterproductive, then we should not help orphans because they've done something in a past life to deserve their present predicament. Whatever feelings of compassion we may naturally feel must be met with a response like, "They're in pain because they *should* be in pain." Furthermore, interference in their anguish is actually unmerciful because it extends their suffering.

On the contrary, we appeal to the Christian belief that all persons are moral agents created in the image of God. Keith Ward provides an excellent appeal to the law of God written on our hearts regarding the problematic morality of samsara:

> The rebirth hypothesis in the end gives an unsatisfactory explanation of the great inequalities of human birth, and has a morally questionable tendency to blame the disadvantaged for their own condition. . . . If my karma must play itself out, then any alleviation of my suffering by another—God or creatures—can only postpone it to another life. . . . In addition to complicating factors based on human freedom in community, the theory of karmic law also stands in tension with much modern scientific understanding of physical causality. Physical and biological laws produce their effects without reference to moral considerations.[41]

Samsara fails morally because it promotes the continuation of human suffering rather than a principled attempt to alleviate it. It

---

41   Keith Ward, *Religion and Human Nature* (Oxford: Clarendon, 1998), 62, 66, 68.

feeds cruelty rather than mercy. The doctrine of rebirth carries no small number of moral and philosophical problems.

On a personal note, the many late nights of studying church and secular history have created a deep-seated (dare I say, heart-pricked) gratitude for the countless Christian men and women who have taken bold stands against evil and corruption. Martin Luther took just such a stand at the Diet of Worms, "Here I stand. I can do no other." Similarly, the prophet Elijah stared down 450 prophets of Baal, whose hearts were hard as iron and whose hands were soaked with sacrificed children's blood; at high noon on Mount Carmel, he was the man of God—and the only one left standing at the end of the day (1 Kings 19). The British blue-blood Parliament member William Wilberforce's efforts also led to the abolition of the British slave trade. Justin Martyr, Tertullian, and other early church fathers lambasted the pagan world for the culturally accepted crimes of pedophilia and infanticide. And British powerhouse preacher Charles H. Spurgeon, in his own latter-nineteenth-century style of apologetics, challenged naysayers, "The God that answers by orphanages, let him be God."[42] One of the many byproducts of the gospel is mercy for those who cannot help themselves.

Because of the generosity of the people of Grace Fellowship: A Church for All Nations, a number of orphanages exist in Southeast Asia that otherwise would not. One particular orphanage, which I was able to visit some time ago, serves only HIV-positive orphans. Interacting with those precious children was tremendously moving. I saw them eating well, receiving proper medical care, and participating in life-skills training, without which they would otherwise have no hope in the world. It was the love of God that moved a group of Christians in South Florida to action. When people's hearts become transformed by the love of Jesus, they cannot help but assist the vulnerable. You see, this is the heart of God. At this point, you may appeal to your Hindu friends, "If you're concerned

42   Charles Richmond Henderson, "Christianity and Children," *Biblical World* 8, no. 6 (1896): 477.

about human rights, you should consider becoming a Christian because the good news of Jesus Christ best informs *why* you have those properly basic moral beliefs. They also expose the fact that Hinduism is morally problematic."

Scenario 3: Buddha, Jesus, and the Four Sights

Siddhartha Gautama was a prince born in what is modern-day Nepal around 623 BC. He grew up in luxury, well isolated from any sort of suffering. One day, venturing outside the bubble of the palace walls, he witnessed an older man (aging), a person ravaged by illness (disease), a funeral procession (death), and a wandering ascetic who seemed happy despite his lack of material goods (want). This experience became known as the "legend of the four passing sights." Visibly shaken, Siddhartha asked, "Is there any realm . . . in which human beings are freed from these facts of human existence?"[43] Thus began the Great Renunciation, in which Siddhartha fled his luxurious life in search of answers to these problems. A question drove his quest: Can anyone escape suffering and death?[44] Siddhartha later became known as the Buddha.

Some contemporary persons may categorize this renunciation by Siddhartha as some sort of freak-out or life-stage-induced meltdown. You can imagine the Twitter comments, "He's lost his mind! What was he smoking?" But the absurdity lies not in the search for answers but in a lifestyle that shrugs its shoulders at the pain, suffering, and death one sees in the world. Numbing ourselves with empty entertainment, with no substantive thoughts about deeper things, may be far more a sign of mental decay than forsaking everything in search of clarity.

So this UCD against Buddhism will be a little different. It's sort of a comparison between Buddha and Jesus rather than an

---

43 Timothy D. Hoare, *Thailand: A Global Studies Handbook* (Santa Barbara, CA: ABC-CLIO, 2004), 133.

44 For a robust assessment of Buddhism, see Keith Yandell and Harold Netland, *Buddhism: A Christian Exploration and Appraisal* (Downers Grove, IL: IVP Academic, 2009).

undercutting of specific Buddhist claims. Given the nature of Buddhist thought, this seemingly modest counter may be more effective. So here it goes—in both short and long forms.

The short UCD: In a fascinating parallel, Jesus also encountered the "four sights" that triggered young Siddhartha's renunciation. Even from his childhood, Jesus had an overwhelming sense of purpose that guided his life. Whereas the four sights led to a worldview crisis within Siddhartha, Jesus simply cured the ill, healed the lame, and raised the dead. Suffering caused the Buddha to seek the safety of enlightenment, whereas Jesus embraced suffering and defeated evil. The writer of the New Testament book of Hebrews puts it this way, "Since therefore the children share in flesh and blood, he himself likewise partook of the same things, that through death he might destroy the one who has the power of death, that is, the devil, and deliver all those who through fear of death were subject to lifelong slavery" (Heb. 2:14–15).

The long UCD: Jesus doesn't seem shaken by the aging process. In the Sermon on the Mount, Jesus asks, "And which of you by being anxious can add a single hour to his span of life? And why are you anxious about clothing? Consider the lilies of the field, how they grow: they neither toil nor spin, yet I tell you, even Solomon in all his glory was not arrayed like one of these. But if God so clothes the grass of the field, which today is alive and tomorrow is thrown into the oven, will he not much more clothe you, O you of little faith?" (Matt. 6:27–30). Notice how Jesus is totally unfazed by these lightning rods of stress. Far from being debilitatingly anxious, Jesus grounds his command to not worry in the nature of a personal, benevolent, and sovereign God. This God cares for the birds of the air, seemingly insignificant flowers, and you and me.

Regarding disease, we should acknowledge Buddha's moral advancement over his Hindu contemporaries, "On another occasion the Buddha discovered a monk whose body was covered with sores, his robe sticking to the body with pus oozing from the sores. Unable to look after him, his fellow monks had abandoned him. On discovering this monk, the Buddha boiled water and washed the monk with his own hands, then cleaned and dried his robes. . . . Thus the Buddha not only advocated the importance of looking after the sick, he also set a noble example by himself ministering to those who were so ill that they were even considered repulsive by others."[45] I think we can all acknowledge the moral praiseworthiness of such actions. We're not saying they're salvific. Rather, Christians and all people of good will should applaud the alleviation of suffering and the promotion of human flourishing.

What did Jesus do when encountering disease? He healed people of their diseases, "And he went throughout all Galilee, teaching in their synagogues and proclaiming the gospel of the kingdom and healing every disease and every affliction among the people. So his fame spread throughout all Syria, and they brought him all the sick, those afflicted with various diseases and pains, those oppressed by demons, epileptics, and paralytics, and he healed them" (Matt. 4:23–24). While Buddha's acts of mercy were an ethical advancement in his day, Jesus showed his superior spiritual power by delivering people from physical and spiritual diseases.

Consider the sight of death, which drove Buddha to a lifelong quest for enlightenment. Jesus overturns death itself. When his friend Lazarus dies, he tells Lazarus's sister, "I am the resurrection and the life. Whoever believes in me, though he die, yet shall he live, and everyone who lives and believes in me shall never die. Do you believe this?" (John 11:25–26). Jesus then stands before the grave and bellows, "Lazarus, come out" (v. 43). Immediately, Lazarus walks out.[46] This isn't the only instance in which Jesus raises the dead. Speaking of Jesus's resurrection, the apostle Paul declares, "When the perishable puts on the imperishable, and the mortal puts on immortality, then shall come to pass the saying that is written: 'Death is swallowed up in victory.' 'O death, where is your victory? O

---

45 "Ministering to the Sick and the Terminally-Ill," *Collected Bodhi Leaves*, vol. 5, *Numbers 122 to 157* (Kandy, Sri Lanka: Buddhist Publication Society, 2012), 141.

46 The text doesn't say whether the family received a refund from the funeral director, so we can only wonder.

death, where is your sting?' The sting of death is sin, and the power of sin is the law. But thanks be to God, who gives us the victory through our Lord Jesus Christ" (1 Cor. 15:54–57). Do you see the difference? Buddha tried to seek an escape from the constraints of morality, whereas Jesus conquers death itself.

Regarding want, Jesus says, "Foxes have holes, and birds of the air have nests, but the Son of Man has nowhere to lay his head" (Luke 9:58). Jesus lays aside the riches of heaven, not in a quest to find himself or solve enigmas about the universe, but to offer salvation to all who would believe in him. The apostle Paul comments on Jesus's divine rescue mission, "For our sake he made him to be sin who knew no sin, so that in him we might become the righteousness of God" (2 Cor. 5:21).

At this point, we see a significant contrast between Buddha and Jesus. Where Buddha seeks answers, Jesus says, "I am the way, and the truth, and the life. No one comes to the Father except through me" (John 14:6). We find in Jesus what is absent in Buddha: absolute confidence and authority. Jesus sees the same sights but delivers people from them (e.g., disease) or outright conquers them (e.g., death). This is true boss status. Jesus carries himself like someone who owns the place. He's not an explorer seeking enlightenment, but a man on a rescue mission. The apostle John explains, "The reason the Son of God appeared was to destroy the works of the devil" (1 John 3:8). If you're going to allow a place for spirituality in your worldview, why not go with this guy? If you are seeking spiritual insight, would it not make better sense to lean in more toward Jesus than Buddha?

What do we find in Jesus that we don't find in Buddha? We find salvation in a personal Savior. Granted, Buddhists generally do not consider Buddha a salvific figure, nor do they see this as a shortcoming. But wouldn't a savior be better than a mere teacher? We find salvation through faith in Jesus because of his absolute authority over all things, including the power of death. Buddha teaches that the key is to change your state of mind. In other words, look within. Jesus warns us that looking within is like trying to find life inside a dried-up sepulcher (Matt. 23:27). Jesus says, "For from within, out of the heart of man, come evil thoughts, sexual immorality, theft, murder, adultery, coveting, wickedness, deceit, sensuality, envy, slander, pride, foolishness. All these evil things come from within, and they defile a person" (Mark 7:21–23). The answers to the problems of the world aren't found inside of us. Far from it! Jesus says something Buddha never would, "Come to me, all who labor and are heavy laden, and I will give you rest" (Matt. 11:28). Notice Jesus's clarity: he and he alone is the burden-bearer and rest-giver.

Again, this is boss-level stuff. Buddha merely teaches, but Jesus delivers. Where Buddha suggests, "be ye lights unto yourselves,"[47] Jesus declares, "I am the light of the world. Whoever follows me will not walk in darkness, but will have the light of life" (John 8:12). The intellectual thrust of Buddha's philosophy was "to wonder about the inescapability of suffering and death."[48] Jesus's good news centers on his willing embrace of and ability to conquer suffering and death for us through his resurrection from the dead.

47   John C. Plott, *Global History of Philosophy* (Delhi, India: Motilal Banarsidass, 1987), 1:90.

48   Lawrence S. Cunningham and John J. Reich, *Culture and Values: A Survey of the Humanities*, 6th ed. (Belmont, CA: Thomson Wadsworth, 2006), 1:175.

CHAPTER 5

THE HISTORICAL JESUS AND THE COMPETITION

Why is the historical Jesus important? Luke Timothy Johnson explains, "Simply as the pivotal figure in the shaping of Western culture, the human being Jesus must be engaged. Ignorance of Jesus when studying the character of European or American civilization is as inexcusable as omitting consideration of Muhammad in seeking to understand the culture of the Middle East, or skipping over Confucius when trying to grasp Chinese culture."[1] In the world of comparative religions, the historical Jesus is an anomaly. Not only is Jesus almost universally accepted as a real historical figure, but in terms of manuscript evidence, he far outmatches every other religious founder to such a degree that there is simply no comparison.[2] To see this clearly, we look to the deep gap of historical data between Jesus and the founders or figures of other major world religions. The sheer magnitude of raw information on Jesus is astonishing, both in terms of volume and precision, compared to that of Krishna, Buddha, and

---

1   Luke Timothy Johnson, "Learning the Human Jesus: Historical Criticism and Literary Criticism," in *The Historical Jesus: Five Views*, eds. James K. Beilby and Paul Rhodes Eddy (Downers Grove, IL: IVP Academic, 2009), 153.

2   Robert M. Price holds that Jesus never existed, but his position is in the extreme minority. For his argument, see "Jesus at the Vanishing Point," in Beilby and Eddy, *Historical Jesus*, 55–104.

Muhammad. Let's take a look at these three figures and see how they measure up against the historical data on Jesus.

The Historical Krishna

Although not a founder per se, Krishna nonetheless ranks as a significant figure in Hinduism. Edwin Bryant recounts, "Early Buddhist sources also provide evidence of the worship of Krishna prior to the Common Era. Whether one looks at the *Nidessa* from the fourth century BC or the *Mahabharata* (dated anywhere from 3100 BC to the fourth century AD), the portrait of Krishna is, at best, hazy."[3] While it is reasonable to conclude that he was a historical figure, the shaky sands of corroborating historiographical and manuscript evidence handicap scholars from establishing anything other than a very vague outline of Krishna's historicity.[4]

Such a lack of solid historical evidence (even for making a minimal facts argument) could spill over into the vagueness of religious practice. Hindu ethics have long been recognized as anything but absolute, especially compared to the main monotheistic religions—Judaism, Islam, and Christianity. As S. S. Rama Rao Pappu observes,

> There is no strict separation between "is" and "ought" in Hindu ethics. . . . The answer to "What ought I to do?" is more complex in Hindu ethics than in the Western religious ethics like Christianity. Of course, a simple but formal answer to this question is, "Do what dharma dictates," or "Do whatever your dharma is." This answer, however, is empty of content. It is like the captain of the team advising his or her players, "Do your best," which cannot guide the players' conduct. Unlike a single scrip-

---

3   Edwin Francis Bryant, *Krishna: A Sourcebook* (New York: Oxford University Press, 2007), 4.

4   R. C. Majumdar argues for the historicity of Krishna, "There is now a general consensus of opinion in favour of the historicity of Krishna." *The History and Culture of the Indian People* (Bombay: Bharatiya Vidya Bhavan, 1951), 1:303.

ture such as the Bible, which is the primary authority in moral matters for Christianity, there is no single book or a single authoritative church in Hinduism to interpret what one's dharma is. Moreover, Hinduism is a pluralistic religion and has no central authority to say conclusively what one ought or ought not to do in moral matters. Each individual is therefore responsible to find out what one's dharma is and act accordingly.[5]

Robust historical data on a religious figure helps solidify the parameters of religious devotion and ethics. An absence of the former could foster a lack of confidence in whether a received religious ritual is even authoritative. Hence, in order to compensate for these historical uncertainties, we should expect a wide girth in religious practice.

The Historical Buddha

A similar problem confronts the scholar who attempts to ascertain with confidence details of the historical Buddha. The Buddhist scriptures were composed hundreds of years after the time in which the Buddha supposedly lived. This is in sharp contrast to the New Testament, which was composed within the lifetime of Jesus's disciples. Hans Penner observes, "The issue here is, 'are the words in the text the words of a historical person?' Clearly, the only sources we have for an answer to that question are late Buddhist texts."[6] Edward Conze, the translator of *Buddhist Scriptures*, laments the deplorable state of trying to reconstruct the historical Buddha:

> Buddhist tradition differs fundamentally from that of Christianity. In Christianity we can distinguish an "ini-

---

5   S. S. Rama Rao Pappu, "Hindu Ethics," in *Contemporary Hinduism: Ritual, Culture, and Practice*, ed. Robin Rinehart (Santa Barbara, CA: ABC-CLIO, 2004), 166, 169.

6   Hans H. Penner, *Rediscovering the Buddha: Legends of Buddha and Their Interpretation* (New York: Oxford University Press, 2009), 128.

tial tradition," embodied in the "New Testament," from a "continuing tradition," which consists of the Fathers and doctors of the Church, the decisions of councils and synods, and the pronouncements of various hierarchies. Buddhists possess nothing that corresponds to the "New Testament." The "continuing tradition" is all that is clearly attested. *The bulk of the selections in this book was written down between A.D. 100 and 400, in other words about 600 to 900 years after the Buddha's demise.* For the first five hundred years the Scriptures were orally transmitted. . . . Different schools wrote down different things. Much of it was obviously composed centuries ago, and some of it must represent the direct and actual sayings of the Buddha himself. At present we have, however, no objective criterion which would allow us to isolate the original gospel. All attempts to find it are based on mere surmise, and the discussion of the subject generally leads to nothing but ill will and fruitless disputes.[7]

In other words, the quest for details on the historical Buddha is a historiographical black hole. There is simply no parallel in Buddhism to the numerous early New Testament manuscripts, early church fathers' writings, early Christian creeds, and enemy attestation. In an exchange with Japanese Buddhists, Paul Tillich posed a historical inquiry about the truth claims of Buddhism, "'If some historian should make it probable that a man of the name Gautama never lived, what would be the consequence for Buddhism?' After noting that the question of the historicity of Gautama Buddha has never been a central issue for Buddhism, one scholar responded by saying, 'According to the doctrine of Buddhism, the *dharma kaya* [the body of truth] is eternal, and so it does not depend upon

---

7   Edward Conze, trans., *Buddhist Scriptures* (New York: Penguin Books, 1959), 11–12 (emphasis mine).

the historicity of Gautama.'"[8] It's tough to imagine a concept more foreign to Christianity. The idea that the founder's historicity makes no ultimate difference to the religion's truth seems, in the words of Vizzini in *The Princess Bride*, "inconceivable!"[9] The New Testament takes it a step further, beyond Jesus's mere historicity: if Jesus was not resurrected, then Christianity collapses (1 Cor. 15).[10] Unlike Buddhism, Christianity's teachings cannot be separated from the historical Jesus.

The Historical Muhammad

Born in the deserts of modern-day Saudi Arabia in the seventh century, the religion of Islam is surprisingly anemic concerning verifiable facts about Muhammad. Of this intriguing evidential gap, Irving M. Zeitlin writes,

> With regard to Muhammad's Meccan period, practically nothing is known for sure except his marriage and his preaching. The Quran itself provides no coherent biographical narrative, and as [F. E.] Peters aptly observes, "For Muhammad, unlike Jesus, there is no Josephus to provide a contemporary political context, no literary apocrypha for a spiritual context and no Qumran scrolls to illuminate a Palestinian 'sectarian milieu.'" . . .
> The original text of Ibn Ishaq's biography was lost, and no extant copy of the original exists. All we have is the

---

8   Keith Yandell and Harold Netland, *Buddhism: A Christian Exploration and Appraisal* (Downers Grove, IL: IVP Academic, 2009), 197–98; citing Robert W. Wood, ed., "Tillich Encounters Japan," *Japanese Religions* 2, nos. 2–3 (1961): 48–50.

9   *The Princess Bride*, directed by Rob Reiner (Culver City, CA: Act III Communications, 1987), 98 mins.

10   "Christian faith, by contrast, is inextricably rooted in the historical person of Jesus so that Christian teachings cannot be separated from his life, death and resurrection." Yandell and Netland, *Buddhism*, 198.

recension by Ibn Hisham who died more than 200 years
after the Hijra. . . . The truth, then, is that the quest for
the historical Muhammad is beset with difficulties and
problems, the chief of which is the nature of the sources.[11]

The primary problem arising from "the nature of the sources" is
that they are from non-eyewitnesses who were far removed by
several generations from the actual events. Unlike the study of the
historical Jesus, which yields mountains of eyewitness testimonies
(as well as enemy attestation) within less than one hundred years
of Jesus's death, there is no comparative manuscript evidence for
the historical Muhammad. On this note, F. E. Peters laments, "The
historicity of the Islamic tradition is . . . to some degree problematic:
while there are no cogent internal grounds for rejecting it, there are
equally no cogent external grounds for accepting it. . . . The only
way out of the dilemma is thus to step outside the Islamic tradition
altogether and start again."[12] Undoubtedly, parallel or contemporary
sources can assist in understanding the historical basis of one's religion. But having to consistently step outside of the primary sources
altogether because of their weakness should be a cause for serious
concern. On the other hand, Christianity suffers no such problem.

The Historical Jesus

Some claim that between the death of Jesus and the composition
of the New Testament, the biblical writers changed Jesus from a
charismatic leader into the Messiah. John Dominic Crossan calls the
30s and 40s of the first century "the lost years of earliest Christianity
. . . those dark ages."[13] While there's usually a market for theories

---

11 Irving M. Zeitlin, *The Historical Muhammad* (Malden, MA: Polity Press,
    2007), 1–2.
12 F. E. Peters, *Muhammad and the Origins of Islam* (Albany: State University of
    New York Press, 1994), 312.
13 John Dominic Crossan, *The Birth of Christianity* (San Francisco: HarperCol-
    lins, 1998), ix; quoted in Paul Barnett, *The Birth of Christianity: The First*

like this on popular-level blogs, it reflects a willful ignoring of the data. Manuscript evidence for Jesus outweighs the evidence for not only every other ancient religious leader but also ancient secular leaders by leaps and bounds. Gary Habermas recounts, "The New Testament is easily the best attested ancient writing in terms of the number of manuscripts. Ancient classical works have comparatively few manuscripts, with twenty entire or partial copies generally being an excellent number. By comparison, the New Testament has more than five thousand copies. Such a wide difference would provide the New Testament with a much better means of textual criticism, which is crucially important in ascertaining the original readings."[14] Habermas's point concerning textual evidence is enormous. Michael Grant argues, "But, above all, if we apply to the New Testament, as we should, the same sort of criteria as we should apply to other ancient writings containing historical material, we can no more reject Jesus' existence than we can reject the existence of a mass of pagan personages whose reality as historical figures is never questioned."[15] Simply put, if we toss Jesus out, we'd be intellectually obligated to discard vast portions of ancient history as well. If Jesus goes down, so does pretty much everyone else. The ungrounded disparity in historical standards should pique our curiosity as to whether there's some other motivation than a quest for knowledge.

Sir Arthur Conan Doyle's genius sleuth, Sherlock Holmes, comments, "Once your point of view is changed, the very thing which was so damning becomes a clue to the truth."[16] This is precisely the

---

Twenty Years (Grand Rapids: Eerdmans, 2005), 1. R. T. France summarizes William Wrede's skeptical claims, "Mark's presentation of Jesus as Messiah was not a development from Jesus' own claim but a falsification of it." "Development in New Testament Christology," Themelios 18, no. 1 (1992): 5.

14 Gary R. Habermas, The Historical Jesus: Ancient Evidence for the Life of Christ (Joplin, MO: College Press, 1996), 54. See F. F. Bruce, The New Testament Documents: Are They Reliable? (Grand Rapids: Eerdmans, 1967), 16.

15 Michael Grant, Jesus: An Historian's Review of the Gospels (New York: Scribner's, 1977), 199–200, quoted in Habermas, Historical Jesus, 36.

16 Sir Arthur Conan Doyle, "The Problem of Thor Bridge," in The Complete Sherlock Holmes (New York: Barnes & Noble Classics, 2003), 594.

point. As we've noted, we all have bias. But when our minds calcify around that bias, we run the risk of missing not merely a historical observation but the point of life itself. If the Jesus of Scripture is indeed the real Jesus of history, then we owe it to ourselves to not run past him. Again, we would do well to heed the cautions of Sherlock Holmes, "It is a capital mistake to theorize before you have all the evidence. It biases the judgment."[17]

General and Special Revelation

At this stage in our discussion, let's discuss the connection and distinction between general and special revelation. Here's why this is important: there are truths about God that we can discover in nature—for example, that he exists. The apostle Paul puts it this way, "For his invisible attributes, namely, his eternal power and divine nature, have been clearly perceived, ever since the creation of the world, in the things that have been made. So they are without excuse" (Rom. 1:20). By the term *general revelation*, I am speaking of access to truth about God as revealed in nature. You may have noticed how often I've used a diverse collection of evidences and reasons to make my case. UCDs are within the sphere of general revelation. We use these tools of God's common grace to gently persuade. I'd like to outline the relevance of general revelation to persuasive apologetics, especially concerning moral values and human rights. As David Baggett and Jerry Walls observe, "The theistic defender of human rights need only argue that respect-for-persons is *best explained* by theism, not *supportable only* on religious grounds. Again, it would be rather unlikely, if this world *were* a theistic one inhabited by creatures made in the image of the eternal God, that absolutely no progress could be made, using the fertile resources of this world, to explain human dignity. The question is whether this world alone can explain it as well as God *and* the world

17   Sir Arthur Conan Doyle, *A Study in Scarlet* (Madison, WI: Cricket House Books, 2010), 23.

can."[18] Ultimately, it's not just theism we need. We need something more—arguably Christian theology—in order to make sense of our best moral intuitions. The theology of Christianity and the special revelation of Scripture give us even more profound reasons to take our moral intuitions and insights seriously.

While I do not wish to oversimplify this complex issue, natural theology does supply a number of moral reference points for Christianity. General revelation can reveal moral law, whereas special revelation provides the identity and character of the lawgiver. General revelation is exactly that—general. Scripture (special revelation), rather than tradition, is the clearest barometer for clarifying our perceived sense of moral truths.[19] But delineating between general and special revelation is far more challenging than it appears at first glance.

Jesus summarizes the law, "You shall love the Lord your God with all your heart and with all your soul and with all your mind. This is the great and first commandment. And a second is like it: You shall love your neighbor as yourself. On these two commandments depend all the Law and the Prophets" (Matt. 22:37–40). Tying this together with the apostle Paul's claim that the law is written on the human heart (Rom. 2:14–15), we gain several insights. First, properly basic moral beliefs find their grounding in the moral law of God available to all persons via the conscience. Second, Jesus's admonition to "love your neighbor as yourself" assumes self-love. Paul recognizes natural self-love when he writes, "For no one ever hated his own flesh, but nourishes and cherishes it" (Eph. 5:29). Self-love is the apex of care, and Jesus and Paul both use it as a call

---

18   David Baggett and Jerry L. Walls, *God and Cosmos: Moral Truth and Human Meaning* (New York: Oxford University Press, 2016), 118–19 (emphasis original).

19   Kevin J. Vanhoozer paraphrases Nicholas Healy's remarks, "Neither tradition nor practice can be the supreme norm for Christian theology, because each is susceptible to error. Practices become deformed; traditions become corrupt." *The Drama of Doctrine: A Canonical Linguistic Approach to Christian Theology* (Louisville: Westminster John Knox, 2005), 22. See Nicholas M. Healy, *Church, World and the Christian Life: Practical-Prophetic Ecclesiology* (Cambridge: Cambridge University Press, 2000), 9–13.

to love others to the same degree. Human rights are in large part recognizing other persons as having inestimable and intrinsic value. Scripture categorically roots this in the belief that God has created every person. Scripture frames treating others well as an extension of how we love ourselves.

Furthermore, general revelation is sufficient for recognizing basic moral beliefs because they are *generally available to humanity as a whole*.[20] On the other hand, special revelation serves to explain further *why* crimes such as sacrificing infants are morally wrong and why protecting toddlers from abuse, even if it costs one's life, is morally praiseworthy. Here's the point: we need special revelation to fill in the outline. General revelation provides the form, and special revelation provides the substance. Both are revelation from God and about God.[21] For instance, following the intricacies of the universe to infer that there is a designer helps us see why it is reasonable to assume that God exists.[22] The first (general revelation) points to a creator, whereas the second (special revelation) leads to the creator's identity. Thus, general and special revelation are thoroughly complementary.[23]

---

20 William Lane Craig, "Doctrine of Revelation (Part 1): Introduction to General Revelation," Reasonable Faith, November 5, 2014, https://www.reasonablefaith.org/podcasts/defenders-podcast-series-3/doctrine-of-revelation-part-1/doctrine-of-revelation-part-1.

21 Louis Berkhof writes, "This distinction between general and special revelation focuses more on the extent and purpose of revelation. General revelation is referred to as 'general' revelation because it has a general content and is revealed to a general audience. Through general revelation to all men, God communicates His existence, His power, and His glory, such that men are left without excuse." *Introduction to Systematic Theology* (Grand Rapids: Eerdmans, 1932), 128; quoted in Keith Mathison, "General and Special Revelation—A Reformed Approach to Science and Scripture," *Ligonier*, May 18, 2012, http://www.ligonier.org/blog/general-and-special-revelation-reformed-approach-science-and-scripture.

22 See the work of my friend and professor William A. Dembski, *The Design Inference: Eliminating Chance through Small Probabilities* (New York: Cambridge University Press, 2006).

23 Article XII of The Chicago Statement on Biblical Inerrancy explains, "We deny that Biblical infallibility and inerrancy are limited to spiritual, religious, or re-

Christian theism weaves both together into a beautiful tapestry of redemption. We often find a healthier environment for human rights, the existence of more advanced laws to protect children, and a foundational respect for the rule of law among both individuals and cultures that have even a rudimentary regard for special revelation (Christian Scripture, the life and work of Jesus of Nazareth, the *imago Dei*, etc.). On the contrary, we frequently discover a higher repression of fundamental human rights (especially for vulnerable persons) among cultures that lack or categorically reject special revelation. There seems to be a general correspondence between a culture's access or response to special revelation and its view of human value. Stated succinctly, general revelation gives some access to these beliefs. Still, special revelation helps chart the *why* behind the *what*—namely, that all persons are worthy of respect, dignity, and have intrinsic value regardless of mental or physical limitations.[24]

So how is all this relevant to the present discussion? Our basic moral sensibilities are so real and substantive that they call for a full exposition, which Christianity supplies. Jesus and Paul provide unparalleled vantage points on basic human rights when compared to other worldviews and religions. Christianity is simply in a class of its own both in explanatory power and incarnational example. Again, I believe our basic moral beliefs lead us to theism and, upon further examination of Scripture and Christian teachings, steer us toward Christianity.

H. P. Owen's "Morality and Christian Theism" is quite helpful in tracing the link from general theism to Christian orthodoxy.[25]

---

demptive themes, exclusive of assertions in the fields of history and science. We further deny that scientific hypotheses about earth history may properly be used to overturn the teaching of Scripture on creation and the flood." "The Chicago Statement on Biblical Inerrancy" (Oakland, CA: International Council on Biblical Inerrancy, 1978), 5, s/TL/Special/ICBI_1.pdf.

24   I am grateful for Dr. Larry Starkey's assistance on this point.

25   H. P. Owen, "Morality and Christian Theism," *Religious Studies* 20, no. 1 (1984): 5–17. See David Baggett, "Morality and Christian Theism," *Moral Apologetics*, June 28, 2017, http://moralapologetics.com/morality-and-christian-theism.

Owen lays three ground rules: all persons have access to what can be loosely termed "natural law"; Christian morality does not lack non-Christian parallel; and moral autonomy must be maintained.[26] Christianity gives virtues and moral principles a new "quality" or "direction" through the person of Jesus and the grace he offers.[27] Christians then imitate the example of Jesus through faith, by reflecting his moral goodness and transformative grace. Jesus is the exemplar of impeccable righteousness that Christians follow, but he is far more than a good example. Owen beautifully paints Christianity's fulfillment of the quest for human goodness, "The ideal of 'the good man' has constantly haunted the human race. Christianity provides the ideal with a perfect embodiment in Christ as God incarnate. And thereby it confers on the pursuit of goodness a wholly new motivation. Thus while Plato held that personal goodness was derived from an 'imitation of' and even 'participation in,' the Forms of value culminating in the Form of the Good, he had no concept of a personal Creator who would confer goodness on his human creatures by evoking their response to his love in becoming one of them."[28]

In summary, Christianity exquisitely personifies our commonsensical moral notions. Yet it goes far beyond and clarifies them in the person of Jesus Christ. Here are some practical ways to tie this into persuasive apologetics. We can use the internal witness of the

---

26 Owen, "Morality and Christian Theism," 5–6. Owen continues, "Moral autonomy is itself a gift that God bestows on men in order that they should respond to him, not by blindly obeying his dictates, but by rationally making his will their own and so fulfilling their status as personal (spiritual) creatures" (6).

27 Owen, "Morality and Christian Theism," 7, 8, 10.

28 Owen, "Morality and Christian Theism," 13. Owen goes on to showcase the centrality of humility in Christianity, "In humility, I think, we reach the most distinctive ingredient in the Christian character. Christian humility cannot be reduced to natural modesty (even when this is interpreted in terms of a reluctance to claim much for one's moral achievements). It cannot even be equated with the theist's natural self-abasement before God as the *mysterium tremendum*. It stems from the realization, so poignantly described by Augustine, that we are saved by the humility of God in living a human life and dying a human death for our sake" (13).

conscience and external witness of nature that God has provided for both the evil and the good. Reference what we all, deep down, know to be true and good. Seek out common ground, but unveil who owns the common ground. Make your case for how Jesus fulfills these noble ideals and gives them, in the words of Owen, a new "quality" and "direction."[29] The two-punch combination of general and special revelation is an intellectually honest and emotionally informed approach. In the words of that great motivational speaker, Matt Foley, "Go for it."[30]

---

29 Owen, "Morality and Christian Theism," 7.
30 Chris Farley, "Matt Foley: Van Down by the River," *Saturday Night Live*, May 8, 1993, https://www.nbc.com/saturday-night-live/video/matt-foley-van-down-by-the-river/3505931.

JESUS AND HOPE

The cultural trend in America today seems to be moving away from the mindset that says, "Give me facts and arguments, and I'll follow the data wherever they lead." Rather, people mainly think in terms of the question, "Is this relevant or meaningful to my life *right now*?" Let me be clear: cultural trends can change our starting point for persuasive apologetics, but not our destination. We can start at the fine-tuning of the universe, morality, human rights, cosmology, or literally any other area. If God exists, then all truth is ultimately his truth. Find common ground and start there. That's what persuasive apologetics is all about. Leverage what you need to leverage, and do what you can with what you have. However, the destination never changes. Repentance from sin and faith in Christ—to the glory of God—are the goal.

In this final chapter, I aim to connect hope to Jesus, not as a rhetorical device for barn-burner sermons but as a substantive anchor for one's intellectual, emotional, and spiritual life. Do you think people need hope? I would assume we would all say yes. Hope is what holds us back from slipping into despair when life hits the proverbial fan. This is not pie-in-the-sky escapism, but the stuff of real life. The incarnation of Jesus provides a fuller picture of the filial and familial relationship between God and the persons he has created. Several inferences from the incarnation are relevant here. First, Jesus chose to identify with a race of morally corrupt beings unable to deliver themselves. Second, Jesus taught that persons are valuable because of what they are, not just because of their horizontal achievements. Third, Jesus identified with and experienced human suffering.

The Incarnation and Hope

In the gospel narratives, the incarnation was ground zero in a life destined for death. Even before his crucifixion, we should remember that Jesus was not unfamiliar with suffering. A brief reading of the Gospels reveals that Jesus's actions toward human suffering were anything but indifferent. He showed mercy to a woman accused of adultery, ministered to the physically disabled, welcomed societal outcasts, ministered to the ill, wept over his friend's death, faced rejection from his own family, felt the pangs of false accusation, experienced betrayal from a close friend, and suffered a tortuous death.[1] Yet in Jesus, we see cruelty and selfishness conquered by compassion.

If Jesus had a knowledge of human suffering through personal experience (rather than through a mere cognitive exercise), then the gravity of his words about these realities deepens tremendously.[2] He did not speak of suffering from an Athenian ivory tower, but from under the iron heel of Roman oppression and fanatical intolerance from a religious establishment that rabidly sought his death. Even the agnostic Albert Camus notes the extraordinary implications of Jesus's death concerning the enigma of evil and suffering, "His solution consisted, first, in experiencing them. The god-man suffers too, with patience. Evil and death can no longer be entirely imputed to him since he suffers and dies. The night on Golgotha

---

1   Matt. 12:46–50; Mark 7:32–34; 14:56; Luke 7:34; 18:39; 22:47–48; 23:1–49; John 8:1–11; 11:35.
2   "Loving us, God does not give us something, but Himself; and giving us Himself, giving us His only Son, He gives us everything." Karl Barth, *Church Dogmatics*, vol. II, part 1, *The Doctrine of God*, trans. G. W. Bromiley, eds. G. W. Bromiley and T. F. Torrance (Peabody, MA: Hendrickson, 2010), 276.

is so important in the history of man only because, in its shadows, the divinity, ostensibly abandoning its traditional privileges, lived through to the end, despair included, the agony of death."[3]

Solidarity with humanity by fully entering the human experience is one salient feature of the incarnation. Jesus entered the fray in human flesh, not in a quasi-angelic form immune to human frailty. He experienced the full range of human temptations while retaining his moral purity.[4] Keith Ward notes, "Perhaps the central distinctive teaching of Christianity is that the Divine shares in creaturely suffering, in order that the material order may be liberated from bondage to selfish desire, and transfigured to share in the life of eternity."[5] This is the death of self-serving pride. It's the proverbial director coming out from his chair and playing the lead part in the drama that leads to the ultimate sacrifice of himself.[6] N. T. Wright puts it well, "What the Gospels offer is not a philosophical explanation of evil, what it is or why it's there, nor a set of suggestions for how we might adjust our lifestyles so that evil will mysteriously disappear from the world, but the story of an *event* in which the living God *deals with it*."[7] Jesus voluntarily

---

3   Albert Camus, *Essais* (Paris: Gallimard, 1965), 444; quoted in Bruce K. Ward, "Prometheus or Cain? Albert Camus's Account of the Western Quest for Justice," *Faith and Philosophy* 8, no. 2 (1991): 203. Also, see Alvin Plantinga, *Warranted Christian Belief* (New York: Oxford University Press, 2000), 487–88.

4   "For certainly no seed ever fell from so fair a tree into so dark and cold a soil." C. S. Lewis, *Miracles: A Preliminary Study* (New York: HarperCollins, 1996), 149. This is one of the main points of the letter to the Hebrews and is eloquently expressed by William L. Lane in his commentary *Hebrews: A Call to Commitment* (Vancouver: Regent College, 2004).

5   Keith Ward, *Religion and Human Nature* (New York: Oxford University Press, 1998), 5.

6   Peter Kreeft and Ronald K. Tacelli, *Handbook of Christian Apologetics* (Downers Grove, IL: InterVarsity, 1994), 150–74.

7   N. T. Wright, *Evil and the Justice of God* (Downers Grove, IL: IVP Books, 2006), 93 (emphasis original). David Baggett and Jerry L. Walls describe the incarnation as "a picture of the divine condescending to take human flesh, one person both wholly divine and wholly human. No greater portrait of integration and rapprochement of the natural and supernatural, God and cosmos, is

subjected himself to physical, mental, emotional, and spiritual pain, culminating in his own death.[8]

The Incarnation and Consolation in the Face of Evil

For Christians, the incarnation and passion of Jesus provide an even deeper consolation in the face of evil. Jesus's hard-hitting sermons on children and the penalties for those who harm them avoid the scythe of Aleksandr Solzhenitsyn's words intended for hypocrites masquerading as moral experts, "Those who have continued to live on in comfort scold those who suffered."[9] On the contrary, Jesus's authoritative conclusion "Unless you repent, you will all likewise perish" mercifully points to the way of deliverance in light of the coming judgment (Luke 13:3). Obedience to Jesus's commands is holistic. Mere verbal confession to a collection of theological abstractions is foreign to the New Testament.[10] In addition to his fulfillment of the Hebrew Scriptures, Jesus's uniqueness is abundantly clear in his prescribed ethical norms that, in the words of L. Rush Bush, "will improve our life if followed, but . . . will crush us if they are rejected and ignored."[11] Jesus's regard for the weak and his mercy to the downcast provide a new paradigm of human-to-human relationships in which love overcomes selfishness.[12]

---

easy to envision." *God and Cosmos: Moral Truth and Human Meaning* (New York: Oxford University Press, 2016), 52–53.

8   See William A. Dembski's treatment on the extent of the cross. William A. Dembski, *The End of Christianity: Finding a Good God in an Evil World* (Nashville: B&H, 2009), 16–22.

9   Aleksandr Solzhenitsyn, *The Gulag Archipelago* (New York: Harper & Row, 1974), 1.

10 In the words of Gordon D. Kaufman, "Believing in God is not simply a matter of the confession of a few words: It involves a reordering of our whole existence in its socio-cultural as well as its individual and personal dimensions." "What Shall We Do with the Bible?," *Interpretation* 25 (1971): 112.

11 L. Russ Bush, *The Advancement: Keeping the Faith in an Evolutionary Age* (Nashville: Broadman & Holman, 2003), 105.

12 Jesus went where others would not and associated with the forgotten. As Gerald L. Borchert comments, "When Jesus went to Jerusalem, he did not

At the cross, we see God's wrath against sin poured out, not on the wicked but on an innocent, voluntary substitute. "Or, as the old evangelistic tract put it, the nations of the world got together to pronounce judgment on God for all the evils in the world, only to realize with a shock that God had already served his sentence."[13] Christians believe the resurrection was necessary for salvation, but incarnation and death are the necessary prerequisites. J. R. R. Tolkien puts it this way, "The Birth of Christ is the eucatastrophe of Man's history. The Resurrection is the eucatastrophe of the story of the Incarnation. This story begins and ends in joy."[14] Alvin Plantinga paints the beautiful brokenness of the passion as follows:

> He was subjected to ridicule, rejection, and finally the cruel and humiliating death of the cross. Horrifying as that is, Jesus, the Word, the son of God, suffered something vastly more horrifying: abandonment by God, exclusion from his love and affection, "My God, my God, why have you forsaken me?" All this to enable human beings to be reconciled to God, and to achieve eternal life. This overwhelming display of love and mercy is not merely the greatest story ever told; it is the greatest story that *could* be told. No other great-making property of a world can match this one.[15]

---

spend his time in elite hostels; nor did he concentrate his ministry merely in the temple or give attention to the rich and famous who could help him politically and financially with his ministry. He concentrated on people in need, which for the elite of society was part of his problem. In this story [John 5] he visited the pool below the temple where the helpless dregs of society lay in a pathetic state." *John 1–11*, New American Commentary 25A (Nashville: B&H, 1996), 231.

13 Wright, *Evil and the Justice of God*, 94.

14 J. R. R. Tolkien, "On Fairy-Stories," ILAS 2350, University of Houston, accessed January 1, 2023, https://uh.edu/fdis/_taylor-dev/readings/tolkien.html, under "Epilogue."

15 Alvin Plantinga, *Where the Conflict Really Lies: Science, Religion, and Naturalism* (New York: Oxford University Press, 2011), 58–59 (emphasis original).

According to Christianity, the incarnation and the resurrection of Jesus are not just the sources of revelation by which we can know God, but a medium through which we can understand our own humanity and find hope for overcoming the destructive pull of our lower desires.[16]

The Resurrection and Hope

I think it is altogether appropriate to offer a few words regarding hope and the resurrection to those among us carrying deep personal scars. Childhood trauma can cause a specific and profound sense of loneliness throughout one's adult life. The resurrection of Jesus is the oasis where hurting persons can find solace amid emotional or physical isolation. Loneliness and bitterness are cancers plaguing the human condition. But according to the biblical account, it was not always this way. According to Genesis 1:31, God's initial creation was "very good." God goes on to provide Adam with the companionship of a wife (2:18–25). Yet human rebellion caused a wedge between God and others (3:1–19).

Where Jesus's incarnation identifies with humanity and bridges the gap of isolation brought about by sin, the resurrection champions Jesus's victory over death, the ultimate separator of all human relationships (2 Tim. 1:10). It also reminds us that Jesus is not merely a figure relegated to the pages of ancient history, but a living person. According to the logic of the apostle Paul, if Jesus is not raised, then death is the final period on the last page of one's life (1 Cor. 15:32). Hope is a phantom mirage in a universe that will one day be stripped of any chance of primitive life as it expands into the horizon of a silent and permanent heat death of zero degrees kelvin.[17] Atheist Bertrand Russell's anguished words are a fitting epitaph:

---

16 Søren Kierkegaard, *Works of Love*, ed. and trans. Howard V. Hong and Edna H. Hong (Princeton, NJ: Princeton University Press, 1995), 84.
17 William Lane Craig, *Reasonable Faith: Christian Truth and Apologetics*, 3rd ed. (Wheaton, IL: Crossway, 2008), 141.

I look out upon the night of nothingness. The revolutions of nebulae, the birth and death of stars, are no more than convenient fictions in the trivial work of linking together my own sensations, and perhaps those of other men not much better than myself. No dungeon was ever constructed so dark and narrow as that in which the shadow physics of our time imprisons us, for every prisoner has believed that outside his walls a free world existed; but now the prison has become the whole universe. There is darkness without, and when I die there will be darkness within. There is no splendour, no vastness, anywhere; only triviality for a moment, and then nothing. Why live in such a world? Why even die?[18]

Yet Russell goes on to give a bizarre pep talk about facing the ultimate absurdity of life with bravery, grounded in "the firm foundation of unyielding despair."[19] On the one hand, he admits that there is no point or purpose in the cosmos. On the other hand, he attempts to salvage some scraps of purpose. Russell tries to build a case for hope on a foundation of sand, but to no avail.

Outside of death-conquering resurrection, the best one could hope for is a temporary web of relationships held together by young life stages and the brilliant but finite interventions of modern medicine. But even these will be permanently shattered when the icy grip of death drags the dead away from the living. If the resurrection did not happen, then hope becomes a vacuous and empty concept at best. Hedonistic amusements are little more than

---

18 Bertrand Russell, *The Autobiography of Bertrand Russell* (New York: Routledge, 2009), 374.

19 This is just short of a wholesale capitulation to nihilism, yet Russell still attempts to establish some sort of happiness-producing modus operandi. Russellian bravery smells a bit like a strategy of philosophical self-medication. Bertrand Russell, "A Free Man's Worship," in *Why I Am Not a Christian*, ed. Paul Edwards (New York: Simon & Schuster, 1957), 107.

momentary distractions from the intrinsic absurdity of life. Yet because Jesus was raised, the apostle Paul could confidently speak of joy even during imprisoned isolation.[20] Such joy is a rational consequence of Christ-centered hope as opposed to pipe-dream, wishful thinking completely unhinged from reality.

Though friendships often begin through mutual interests, the ones that align with eternal values show the best chances of survival. Friendships solely based on trivialities can fade quickly and intensify grief and loneliness, especially when health fails and keeps one from participating in the activities that held them together. On the other hand, the resurrection provides for true camaraderie in fulfilling an eternal goal. Strictly horizontal relationships without an eternal reference point result in loss (Luke 9:23–26). It is helpful to remember that conquering loneliness is not so much trying to fill the void in one's own life, but rather pouring out one's life in service to others (even to the ungrateful and unloving). Jesus goes as far as to say, "For whoever would save his life will lose it, but whoever loses his life for my sake will save it" (v. 24). Loneliness is not conquered by incessant activity, recreation, or entertainment. It is overcome by gospel-centered relationships that naturally flow out of lives invested in Jesus's teachings.

Even in cases when Jesus-focused friendships are nowhere to be had due to illness, death, or persecution, the power of Jesus's resurrection is still able to stave off the attacks of debilitating despair. The resurrection allows persons dealing with childhood trauma to center their focus on Jesus so that he is the anchor of their lives. Though they may be healthy and encouraging, friendships are no longer the primary source of hope and meaning. While imprisoned, the apostle Paul writes, "For [Christ Jesus's] sake I have suffered the loss of all things and count them as rub-

---

20 See Phil. 1:4, 25; 2:2, 17–18, 29; 4:1. A brief survey of Paul's letter to the Philippians yields a powerful portrait of how genuine, gospel-centered friendships can sustain one experiencing the loneliness of unjustified incarceration.

bish, . . . that I may know him and the power of his resurrection, and may share his sufferings, becoming like him in his death" (Phil. 3:8, 10).

The resurrection of Jesus offers a balm for systemic emotional instability. Through times of painful suffering or residual effects of childhood trauma, the reality that Jesus lives has the potential to keep one afloat in the roughest waters. The call of Jesus is to follow him, the lonely one who was "despised and rejected by men, a man of sorrows and acquainted with grief; and . . . one from whom men hide their faces" (Isa. 53:3). Even when experiencing betrayal—as Christ did with Judas (Matt. 26:49) and as the apostle Paul did with "false brothers" (2 Cor. 11:26)—the resurrection is a reminder that loneliness is only temporary. Jesus's finished work is the guarantee of the ultimate reunion for all who will be saved, "He will wipe away every tear from their eyes, and death shall be no more, neither shall there be mourning, nor crying, nor pain anymore, for the former things have passed away" (Rev. 21:4).

Persuasive apologetics calls for arduous efforts from those who have experienced supernatural, transformative grace in order to help those who have lost hope. To those who heed Richard Dawkins's call to openly mock Christians, we remember the words of Tertullian, "If then (as I have elsewhere declared) we Christians are expressly commanded by our Master to love our enemies, whom then have we left to hate?"[21]

Finally, let it be known that the gospel of Jesus offers hope for anyone far from God. The Christian emphasis on dignity and worth

---

21 Tertullian, *The Apology of Tertullian and the Meditations of the Emperor Marcus Aurelius*, trans. W. M. Reeve and Jeremy Collier (London: Newberry House, 1889), 103. Ward writes, "It is friendship with God that transforms lust into love, possessiveness into stewardship, and aggression into creativity" (*Religion and Human Nature*, 164). Spiegel concurs, "Let's not give atheists moral ammunition for their skeptical cannons. Let's demonstrate patience and long-suffering with them" (*The Making of an Atheist: How Immorality Leads to Unbelief* [Chicago: Moody, 2010], 127).

applies no matter the degree of corruption (Matt. 5:45–47). Paul showcases the extent of God's love through Jesus, "For while we were still weak, at the right time Christ died for the ungodly. For one will scarcely die for a righteous person—though perhaps for a good person one would dare even to die—but God shows his love for us in that while we were still sinners, Christ died for us" (Rom. 5:6–8). So if he died for the ungodly that they may be justified, they may freely extend the grace they have freely received, even to their enemies.

Once people truly realize the gravity of their own transgressions in light of an omnipotent, omniscient, benevolent God, prideful demands and intellectual arrogance melt away like fresh snow under a flamethrower. Repentance bows the knee and lowers the uplifted head. Regeneration gives life, and divine grace infuses us with the power to live lives of service and gratitude for the undeserved gift of salvation. The gospel of Jesus Christ has the potential to transform sex addicts, swindlers, and money lovers into *former* sex addicts, swindlers, and money lovers. The apostle Paul reminds Christians in the morally corrupt city of Corinth, "Or do you not know that the unrighteous will not inherit the kingdom of God? Do not be deceived: neither the sexually immoral, nor idolaters, nor adulterers, nor men who practice homosexuality, nor thieves, nor the greedy, nor drunkards, nor revilers, nor swindlers will inherit the kingdom of God. And such were some of you. But you were washed, you were sanctified, you were justified in the name of the Lord Jesus Christ and by the Spirit of our God" (1 Cor. 6:9–11). Sinners of all stripes and victorious believers alike can take comfort in the responsiveness of the risen Jesus. As Charles Spurgeon puts it so beautifully, "Our Lord and Master hears with joy the shout of a believer who has vanquished his enemy and, at the same hour, He inclines His ear to the despairing wail of a sinner who has given up all confidence in self and desires to be saved by Him. At one moment He is accepting the crown that the warrior brings Him from the well-fought fight, and at another moment He is healing the brokenhearted and binding up their wounds."[22] Followers of Jesus should resist the temptation of being roped into a game of "Who's right?" rather than a search for "What's right?" Instead, in sincere humility, let us reach out to those dangling from the cliff of despair. As Robert Jastrow famously declares, "For the scientist who has lived by his faith in the power of reason, the story ends like a bad dream. He has scaled the mountains of ignorance; he is about to conquer the highest peak; as he pulls himself over the final rock, he is greeted by a band of theologians who have been sitting there for centuries."[23] In other words, the scientist, steeped in skepticism, wasted so much time coming to the conclusion that the theologians did much earlier. Namely, that there is, in the words of Francis Schaeffer, "the God who is there."[24] Wise persons proportion their belief based on facts, no matter the extent to which those facts challenge entrenched individual or cultural beliefs.[25]

When we allow Scripture to speak, when we are confronted with truths and challenged to consider issues from God's perspective, *as revealed in his Word*, we will *all* feel a bit uncomfortable. Sometimes those truths sting. However, our intent is never to hurt or embarrass, but rather to simply be honest about what Scripture *actually* teaches. Don't tune God out. Know that you're not in this alone because God's Word challenges *all* of us. Here's one thing

---

22 Charles H. Spurgeon, *Finding Peace in Life's Storms* (New Kensington, PA: Whitaker House, 1997), 107–8.

23 Robert Jastrow, *God and the Astronomers* (New York: Norton, 1992), 107.

24 Francis Schaeffer, *The God Who is There: The Complete Works of Francis A. Schaeffer: A Christian Worldview* (Westchester, IL: Crossway Books, 1982), Logos Library System.

25 David Hume writes, "A wise man, therefore, proportions his belief to the evidence." David Hume, *An Enquiry concerning the Human Understanding and an Enquiry concerning the Principles of Morals* (New York: MacMillan & Co, 1894), 110. Norman Geisler counters, "What Hume seems to overlook is that wise people base their beliefs on facts, not simply on odds" ("Miracles and the Modern Mind," in *In Defense of Miracles: A Comprehensive Case for God's Action in History*, eds. R. Douglas Geivett and Gary R. Habermas [Downers Grove, IL: IVP Academic, 1997], 79).

that will follow: every single one of us, from every background, neighborhood, life stage, or socioeconomic situation, will at some point and in some way be confronted with truth that is tough to hear. God loves every single one of us so much, and he reveals his love by calling us to walk his path, which may be brand new compared to everything we've ever felt or been told. No matter your past or present persuasion, know this: there has never been a person alive (except for Jesus) who has not needed God's grace to transform some aspect of his or her life. We all live in a broken world. We're all in need of redemption. We *can* all come to Jesus, the equal-opportunity Savior.